W9-BHE-363

EMPLOYEE SUGGESTION SYSTEMS
Boosting Productivity and Profits

Robert L. Bassford, MBA
Charles L. Martin, Ph.D.

A FIFTY-MINUTE™ SERIES BOOK

CRISP PUBLICATIONS, INC.
Menlo Park, California

EMPLOYEE SUGGESTION SYSTEMS
Boosting Productivity and Profits

Robert L. Bassford, MBA
Charles L. Martin, Ph.D.

CREDITS
Managing Editor: **Kathleen Barcos**
Editor: **Carol Henry**
Typesetting: **ExecuStaff**
Cover Design: **Carol Harris**
Artwork: **Ralph Mapson**

All rights reserved. No part of this book may be reproduced or transmitted in any form or by any means now known or to be invented, electronic or mechanical, including photocopying, recording, or by any information storage or retrieval system without written permission from the author or publisher, except for the brief inclusion of quotations in a review.

Copyright © 1996 by Crisp Publications, Inc.

Printed in the United States of America by Bawden Printing Company.

Distribution to the U.S. Trade:

National Book Network, Inc.
4720 Boston Way
Lanham, MD 20706
1-800-462-6420

Library of Congress Catalog Card Number 96-85016
Bassford, Robert and Charles Martin
Employee Suggestion Systems
ISBN 1-56052-395-6

This book is printed on recyclable paper with soy ink.

LEARNING OBJECTIVES FOR:

EMPLOYEE SUGGESTION SYSTEMS

The objectives for *Employee Suggestion Systems* are listed below. They have been developed to guide you, the reader, to the core issues covered in this book.

Objectives

- ☐ 1) **To point out benefits of an Employee Suggestion System**

- ☐ 2) **To explain how to set up an Employee Suggestion System**

- ☐ 3) **To discuss promotion ideas for an Employee Suggestion System**

- ☐ 4) **To present ways to avoid problems with Employee Suggestion Systems**

Assessing Your Progress

In addition to the Learning Objectives, *Employee Suggestion Systems* includes a unique new **assessment tool**,* which can be found at the back of this book. A twenty-five item, multiple choice/true-false questionnaire allows the reader to evaluate his or her comprehension of the subject matter covered. An answer sheet, with a chart matching the questions to the listed objectives, is also provided.

* Assessments should not be used in any selection process.

ABOUT THE AUTHORS

Robert L. Bassford, MBA

Robert is the owner of Baston Consulting, a firm that advises clients in the areas of cost containment and employee suggestion systems. He designs and implements employee suggestion systems, which have saved his clients millions of dollars. Robert is a trainer in creativity and idea generation techniques, and has extensive experience in the field of new product development. Robert is a U.S. patent holder. He received his MBA from Wichita State University. You can contact Mr. Bassford at 316-683-2718.

Charles L. Martin, Ph.D.

After earning a Ph.D. in marketing from Texas A&M University (1986), Charles L. Martin joined the faculty at Wichita State University, where he is currently an Associate Professor. Dr. Martin has pioneered two courses at WSU focusing upon the marketing challenges faced by service organizations. His interest in service organizations has also translated into an ongoing research program examining the processes service businesses utilize to cement relationships with their customers. To date, Dr. Martin has published 10 books, including *Facilitation Skills for Team Leaders,* Crisp Publications, and more than 170 articles for both trade and academic audiences.

ABOUT THE SERIES

With over 200 titles in print, the acclaimed Crisp 50-Minute™ series presents self-paced learning at its easiest and best. These comprehensive self-study books for business or personal use are filled with exercises, activities, assessments, and case studies that capture your interest and increase your understanding.

Other Crisp products, based on the 50-Minute books, are available in a variety of learning style formats for both individual and group study, including audio, video, CD-ROM, and computer-based training.

Dedication—To my loving, creative wife, Christi. RLB

CONTENTS

CONTENTS (continued)

INTRODUCTION

During the past few years, three important trends have spotlighted and to some extent redefined the role of employees in corporate America. One is the improved education level of typical workers. Rather than simply implementing management's directives in a robotic, thoughtless way, employees today want their contributions to be more meaningful.

Driven by competitive pressures and rising customer expectations, the other two trends are the challenges to control costs while simultaneously improving the quality of products and services. Central to both of these challenges is the philosophy of *continuous improvement*—the ongoing search for a better, more productive way.

The convergence of these three trends has prompted more and more organizations to look to employees for ideas on trimming costs, boosting productivity, improving quality and enriching jobs. Corporate America now recognizes that employees who are invested in their workplace often make better decisions and more substantive contributions. They are also more likely to be committed to those decisions and initiatives if they play an active role in shaping them.

Traditional methods of tapping employees' idea banks and otherwise involving and motivating them have ranged from informal sensing sessions, feedback meetings and open-door policies, to more empowering approaches such as quality circles and self-managed teams, minibusiness units, gainsharing and employee ownership. These techniques work well together and have had measurable success. Still, if your organization has already implemented these approaches and is ready to try something different, or if your company has encountered only limited success with previous efforts to involve employees, consider developing an *employee suggestion system* (ESS). Thousands of organizations—large and small—already have. This book will show you how.

P A R T

I

The Improvement Movement

THE POWER OF IDEAS: BILLION$ $AVED!

More than two billion dollars are saved each year by organizations that solicit improvement ideas from their employees through formal suggestion systems. On average, these companies save more than $33,000 annually per 100 eligible employees.

Many companies attribute advances in quality and innovation to their employee suggestion systems. For example, one major airplane manufacturer incorporated no less than 1,250 employee ideas in designing one of its latest and largest planes. Benefits and savings are realized, as well, by organizations, divisions and departments that have implemented informal, less structured suggestion programs.

Despite these enormous gains, however, the potential for further fattening the bottom line with employees' ideas is still tremendous.

Not a Sick Idea After All!

TYPE OF ORGANIZATION: Hospital

EMPLOYEE IDEA: Reprocess and reuse pulse oximetry sensors instead of throwing them away after one use.

BENEFIT: Eliminates the cost of disposing of and replacing 12,500 sensors.

COST SAVINGS: $120,000 per year

The types of organizations successfully using employee suggestion systems (ESSs) range from private and public for-profit companies, to governmental agencies and nonprofit organizations of all sizes.

If your organization does not have a system in place to harvest and manage the improvement ideas of your employees, or if you have an ineffective program, then you are missing the benefit of a vast, untapped resource. Without a formal system, most improvement ideas will be lost within the organization and never receive the attention and resources they require to bear fruit.

THE POWER OF IDEAS: BILLION$ $AVED! (continued)

Who Benefits

Every organization can benefit from the input of its employees. The key lies in how effectively that input is managed. The flow of improvement ideas will always benefit from having an ESS to gather, evaluate and implement employee ideas. A suggestion system can be customized to fit your organization's needs. It can be simple and require few resources, or it can be sophisticated and use a computer system for detailed tracking and reporting. It can be implemented throughout the entire organization or used within individual departments.

If you want to improve your organization by enhancing the flow of improvement ideas, this book is for you! Here you will learn how to create a system that will

- Teach employees how to make improvements

- Encourage employees to submit improvement ideas

- Channel ideas to the appropriate expert for evaluation

- Track and monitor all ideas being considered

- Communicate results of evaluation to employees in a timely manner

- Distribute approved ideas throughout the organization

- Report results to management

- Reward employees

- Improve employee morale and commitment to the organization

Bank on This Idea

TYPE OF ORGANIZATION: Bank

EMPLOYEE IDEA: Replace paper envelopes used in drive-up windows with reusable plastic containers.

BENEFIT: Eliminates the cost and waste of more than 2 million paper envelopes per year.

COST SAVINGS: $23,000 per year.

BENEFITS OF EMPLOYEE SUGGESTION SYSTEMS

The investment of time, money, people and other resources in designing and implementing an employee suggestion system can reap almost unlimited returns. Indeed, ESSs represent a win-win-win-win proposition: The organization, its employees, its customers, and its investors all benefit. Here are some of the many rewards reported by organizations using an ESS.

Benefits for the Organization

▶ *Reduced costs.* Examples: Lower utility bills by using equipment more efficiently. Reduce the cost of supplies by finding more competitive vendors. Decrease overtime by improving scheduling practices.

▶ *Increased revenues.* Examples: Charge for services previously given away. Open new markets for current products. Generate ideas for new products and services.

▶ *Redefined processes.* Examples: Reduce the number of steps needed to produce products or perform services. Eliminate or decrease manual labor in a process.

▶ *Improved quality.* Workers closest to the task can often identify possibilities for improvement that may not be apparent to management or other employees.

▶ *Increased profits.* Reduced costs, increased revenues and improved quality translate into greater profits.

▶ *Heightened communications.* Organizations are more productive when the channels of communication are working properly. A formal system to collect, evaluate and implement improvement ideas prompts workers to talk with their supervisors and with one another about their job tasks and how to improve them.

▶ *Less resistance to change.* Employees who are creating the changes are more likely to embrace the changes themselves.

▶ *Application of best practices throughout the organization.* A central hub through which all improvement ideas must flow allows the best ideas to be shared throughout the organization. All departments can benefit from widely applicable improvements.

Benefits for Employees

► *Improved morale.* Employees want to be heard. They want to participate in matters that affect them and shape their jobs.

► *Greater cooperation.* As workers come together to jointly develop and fine-tune ideas, a sense of teamwork and cooperation emerges.

► *Tangible rewards.* Suggestion programs can reward employees with cash, merchandise, travel, and days off for their contributions. These rewards may be in direct proportion to the contribution made by the employee's idea.

► *Nonmonetary recognition.* Employees can be recognized both verbally and in writing. Recognizing them in front of their supervisors and peers is a morale booster.

► *Increased creativity.* When employees are asked to share their suggestions, trained to generate improvement ideas, and given an atmosphere that encourages improvement, they will become much more creative.

► *Less rework.* Rework is no fun. Employees can find ways of improving their work processes, so they ultimately have to deal with fewer reworks.

► *Professional development.* Workers who routinely consider ways to improve the company's performance and their own productivity have a broader perspective of their jobs and develop a more thorough understanding of the company. This helps groom them for positions of greater responsibility.

► *Greater job security.* Suggestions from a more knowledgeable, creative, and alert workforce elevate productivity and profitability. This strengthens the organization and creates new opportunities, leading to greater job security.

BENEFITS OF EMPLOYEE SUGGESTION SYSTEMS (continued)

Benefits for Customers

Enhanced customer satisfaction is the bottom line for customers. Employee suggestions can produce higher quality, faster service, new products and services, and lower prices—and thus greater overall perceived value for customers.

Benefits for Investors

Greater return on investment—that's the net effect of suggestions that slash costs, improve quality, boost revenues and enhance customer satisfaction. A fattened bottom line makes investors happy, too!

Ideas to Build On

TYPE OF ORGANIZATION: Construction Company

EMPLOYEE IDEA: Cancel the lease of a radio channel that is little used since cellular phones were purchased.

BENEFIT: Eliminates the monthly payment for a service that is not needed.

COST SAVINGS: $5,000 per year

The following pages illustrate how ESSs increase the odds of a workable idea's survival. An idea must pass through a battery of organizational sieves that can block the flow from creation to implementation. These destructive sieves include:

- Negativity

- Neglect

- Apathy

- Fear

- Lack of Creativity

- Absence of Accountability

Work to eliminate the bottlenecks
where improvement ideas get stuck!

Idea Flow Without *an ESS*

As you read this chart and the chart on the next page, notice what a difference attitude makes in the entire employee suggestion process. Without a formal program, the old, tired business-as-usual attitude prevails.

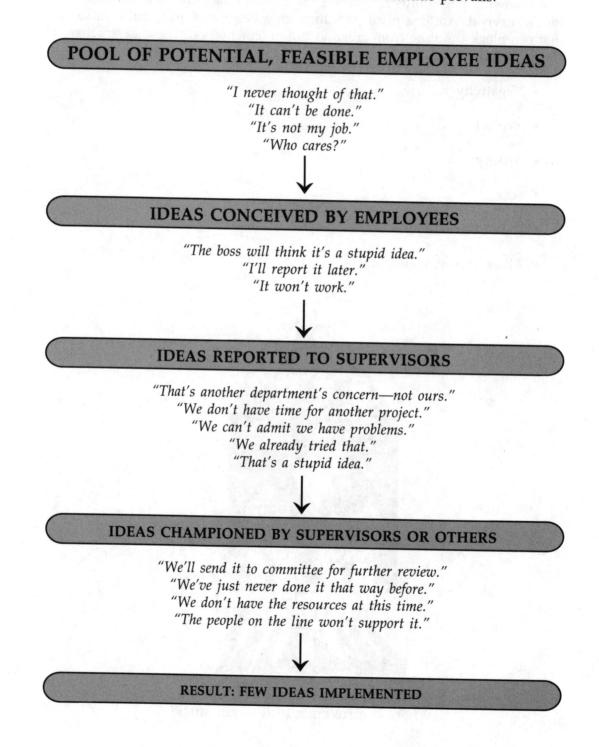

POOL OF POTENTIAL, FEASIBLE EMPLOYEE IDEAS

"I never thought of that."
"It can't be done."
"It's not my job."
"Who cares?"

IDEAS CONCEIVED BY EMPLOYEES

"The boss will think it's a stupid idea."
"I'll report it later."
"It won't work."

IDEAS REPORTED TO SUPERVISORS

"That's another department's concern—not ours."
"We don't have time for another project."
"We can't admit we have problems."
"We already tried that."
"That's a stupid idea."

IDEAS CHAMPIONED BY SUPERVISORS OR OTHERS

"We'll send it to committee for further review."
"We've just never done it that way before."
"We don't have the resources at this time."
"The people on the line won't support it."

RESULT: FEW IDEAS IMPLEMENTED

Idea Flow With *an ESS*

With a formal employee suggestion system, the employees and their ideas are championed by a positive "Yes, why not!" attitude.

POOL OF POTENTIAL, FEASIBLE EMPLOYEE IDEAS

"If I keep working with it, I'll find a solution!"
"Surely, there's a way to do it better?"
"Let's brainstorm!"

↓

IDEAS CONCEIVED BY EMPLOYEES

"What if we did it this way instead?"
"There's no harm in trying."
"The boss will listen."

↓

IDEAS REPORTED TO SUPERVISORS OR ESS OFFICE

"Let's work the numbers and see if it will work."
"We can take a leadership role on this issue."
"It's in everyone's best interest."

↓

IDEAS CHAMPIONED BY SUPERVISORS

"We can't afford not to try it."
"Let's get on it right away."
"What have we got to lose?"

↓

**RESULT:
MANY IDEAS
IMPLEMENTED**

Does Your Organization Need an Employee Suggestion System (ESS)?

Answer the following ten questions about your organization and employees' ideas. Check Yes or No in the appropriate box.

	Yes	No
1. Does your organization have a steady, uninhibited flow of improvement ideas from employees?	☐	☐
2. Do you regularly receive improvement ideas from your employees that effect the bottom line of your organization?	☐	☐
3. Are you confident that employees are actively searching for improvement ideas and otherwise thinking about ways to increase productivity, quality and customer satisfaction?	☐	☐
4. Do employees fully utilize their creative and analytical abilities to generate workable improvement ideas?	☐	☐
5. Are you confident that potentially useful ideas are never stifled by employees or supervisors?	☐	☐
6. Is there a designated place or person employees can contact for help in generating or fine-tuning ideas?	☐	☐
7. Is someone in the organization specifically charged with the responsibility of systematically collecting, screening, analyzing and implementing employee suggestions?	☐	☐
8. Does your organization have a policy that ensures consistent rewards and recognition for employees to make improvements?	☐	☐
9. Is there a system in place to monitor actual performance of implemented improvements?	☐	☐
10. Are employees truly encouraged to submit improvement ideas?	☐	☐

If you answered No to one or more of the above questions, then your company could benefit by soliciting the ideas of your employees through an ESS, or by re-energizing or formalizing your current system. Thousands of organizations have done so during the past decade and are reaping the rewards.

WHY ASK EMPLOYEES FOR SUGGESTIONS?

Ideas can come from a number of sources—including management, customers, consultants, suppliers, trade associations, market researchers, R&D professionals, competitors and universities, to name a few. Indeed, the most successful organizations are learning machines; they gather ideas wherever they can find them.

Employees represent a particularly rich pool of ideas. The vital roles workers play in the organization, coupled with their unique vantage point, offer many benefits to organizations that encourage and cultivate employees' improvement ideas. Consider the following examples:

▶ Employees are in an excellent position to recognize possible improvements. Employees are often the best source for improvement ideas because they are closest to the work. They are familiar with the daily problems and inefficiencies in their jobs. Managers are often too far removed from a particular job or process to know how it might be done better.

▶ Employees bring the best practices from previous employers. Among the most effective employee suggestions are those that recommend changes based on methods used by their former employers.

▶ Employees are able to spot the wasteful practices in their jobs and departments. Managers might see only reports, but workers see the actual wasted time and materials that are being lost every day.

▶ Ideas have power—often even a more powerful impact than is first recognized. One good idea can trigger another and then another.

▶ Shared good ideas have multiple effects. Although employees may be challenged and empowered individually to improve their jobs, improvements must be systematically disseminated throughout the organization to maximize their benefits. Encouraging employees to speak up is the first step.

▶ Suggesting ideas is addictive. Once employees begin to share their ideas, it becomes easier for them to do so in the future. A rewarding experience with one suggestion generally leads to additional ones.

▶ Employees accept self-generated change better than forced change. If they are the ones who suggest the changes, they are less resistant to change and improvement. Even when they are justifiably unhappy with company changes, the ESS provides a consistent mechanism (and challenge) for finding a better way.

THREE FUNDAMENTAL PRINCIPLES OF ESSs

Successful suggestion systems are based on three fundamental principles. Keep them in mind as you build a new ESS or reenergize your current one.

1. Everything Can Be Improved

2. Every Person Is Capable of Generating Improvement Ideas

3. A Formal System Is Required to Best Manage Ideas

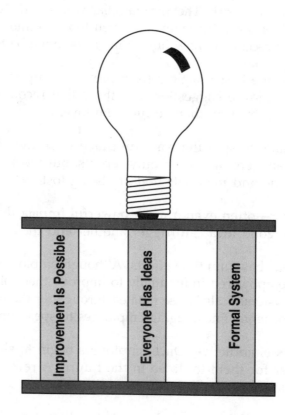

PRINCIPLE #1: Everything Can Be Improved

Believing that everything can be improved, which is also a premise of the quality movement, is critical to the success of any ESS. Advances in technology, innovations by competitors, and increasingly demanding customers all drive the engine of improvement. What was good enough five years or five months ago may be unacceptable today.

Moreover, to foster advancement, the corporate culture must not only accept innovations but must embrace innovative improvements as part of the corporate identity. Improvement should not be "something that we do," but "something that we are." If workers do not believe that there is a better way to do something, they probably will not scrutinize the current method in search of a better way.

If you're not convinced that everything can be improved, try to think of five practices in your organization that are done exactly the same way today as they were a decade ago:

1. _____

2. _____

3. _____

4. _____

5. _____

If you are like most folks, it's likely that you found it difficult to complete the list—despite the thousands of tasks performed in your business. Even if you did think of five things, do a quick review. Some or all of them probably should have already been changed but, for some reason, have not.

THREE FUNDAMENTAL PRINCIPLES OF ESSs (continued)

PRINCIPLE #2: Everyone Is Capable of Generating Improvement Ideas

Some people seem to come up with more ideas than others. They may seem more creative, more insightful, more whatever—but idea generaters are made, not born. With a little training, practice and motivation, everyone can think of potentially useful improvement ideas. The changes may help the company design new products or services. They may affect the way existing products are made, or services and job tasks performed. The improvements may help customers use company products in new, different ways. (For instance, how many people today use baking soda just for baking?)

Most people are surprised at the number of ideas they can generate once they get started and apply themselves. For example, by yourself or with a small group, brainstorm as many alternative uses as you can for an ordinary pencil. List the uses in the spaces below. Let your imagination go wild and allow the alternatives to cover a wide range—how about snack food for pet beavers? Phone dialing devices for fingerless callers?

1. _____

2. _____

3. _____

4. _____

5. _____

6. _____

7. _____

If you thought of a way to use a pencil other than writing, congratulations— you are creative.

In much the same way, there are alternative ways to perform most job tasks. But if no one makes a conscious effort to consider the options, the process of innovation and improvement is greatly slowed.

PRINCIPLE #3: A Formal System Is Required to Best Manage Ideas

Under a formal system of management, improvement ideas are more likely to be identified, considered fairly and implemented. This occurs for a variety of reasons.

▶ An ESS office helps to train and sensitize workers to the potential of improvement ideas, and how to identify them.

▶ Employees know their ideas are welcome. Fears that ideas may be ignored, ridiculed or stolen are put to rest.

▶ Employees have a process to handle their improvement ideas—how to report them and where to submit them.

▶ Ideas are championed. Every idea needs to be promoted by someone who will be involved in the idea's development from conception to fruition. An ESS allows employees to be involved with their ideas from the start. Suggestions therefore don't fall through the cracks or get passed on to less-interested parties for evaluation and development.

▶ Resources are committed. A formal system provides resources earmarked for developing ideas.

▶ An ESS ensures that ideas are not blocked by opponents or stifled by neglect. There is less likelihood of ideas being blocked, ignored, discounted, or forgotten. The formal system presents each idea to pertinent people within the organization and creates a paper trail of the fair and prompt consideration of each idea.

There's No Such Thing as "Penny" Candy!

TYPE OF ORGANIZATION: Chain of retail drug stores

EMPLOYEE IDEA: Place a small coin box next to bulk candy rack, with a sign that requests customers to pay 10 cents for any candy they eat while shopping.

BENEFIT: The store collects money for candy that otherwise would not be paid for. Customers can sample candy while they shop without feeling guilty about not paying.

ADDITIONAL REVENUE: $250,000 per year

P A R T

II

Building Your Suggestion System

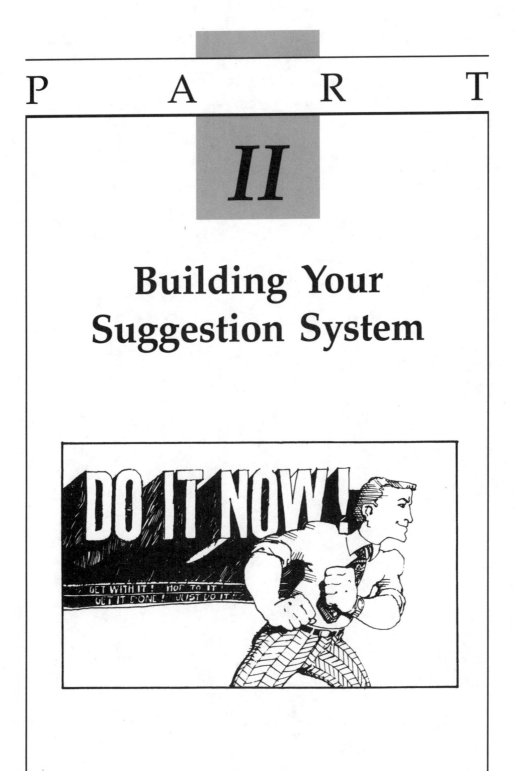

SETTING UP THE SUGGESTION SYSTEM

This next section covers the specific details of developing and implementing the employee suggestion system in most organizations. Of course, it is not necessary that the entire organization implement an ESS. Individual divisions or departments can start their own ESS and build support for company-wide implementation.

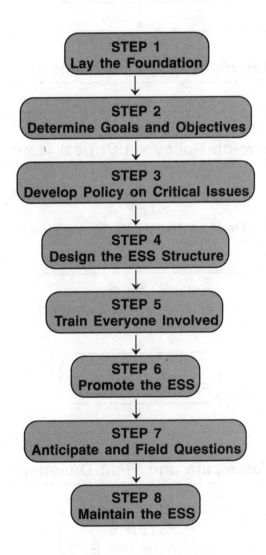

STEP 1
Lay the Foundation

STEP 2
Determine Goals and Objectives

STEP 3
Develop Policy on Critical Issues

STEP 4
Design the ESS Structure

STEP 5
Train Everyone Involved

STEP 6
Promote the ESS

STEP 7
Anticipate and Field Questions

STEP 8
Maintain the ESS

STEP 1: LAY THE FOUNDATION

Laying the foundation for the ESS involves gaining executive management's support and then selecting a steering committee and system administrator.

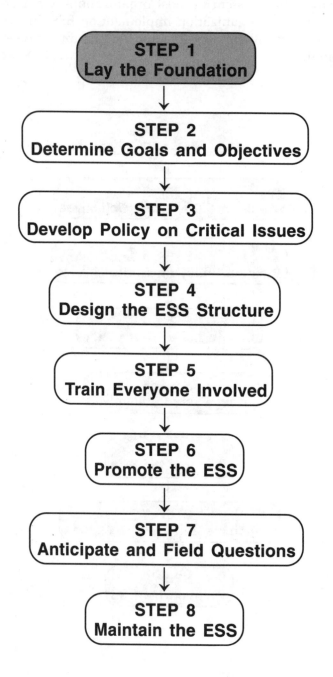

GAINING THE SUPPORT OF EXECUTIVE MANAGEMENT

This is one of the most critical issues in the construction of a formal ESS. Without management support, the ESS is doomed to failure before it is even launched. The work to be done in preparation for the start of the suggestion system will require executive-level support, and so will establishing and staffing the ESS office. Employees' suggestions will require management approval and support for implementation, and, of course, approval of funds for the ESS budget, as well as award payments, come from management.

▶ Employees with ideas will look for signals of management support before they "buy into" the ESS concept.

▶ Supervisors, too, may take a wait-and-see attitude before hyping the ESS in their respective departments.

▶ People in the organization who are asked to evaluate or implement ideas also may look to executive management before investing their time and energy in the ESS. Expect questions such as "Is this ESS stuff permanent or just another passing fad?" "Do they really want our ideas?" "Will they really pay for the good ideas?"

In short, no one will take the ESS seriously if management doesn't.

To begin, schedule a meeting of managers from each major area of the organization.

- Discuss the possibility of starting a suggestion program.

- Quiz them with the ten questions in Part I (page 9).

- Share the success stories illustrated throughout this book.

- Show the group how an ESS is consistent with the company's commitment to quality improvement.

- Point out that a few good ideas—or even just one—is enough to pay for the entire program.

- Respond to their questions and concerns.

- Gauge their level of support on the spot.

- Ask for their commitment, or offer to follow-up with details in another meeting, or with a written proposal.

GAINING THE SUPPORT OF EXECUTIVE MANAGEMENT (continued)

Remember that although initial support is crucial, it is also important to maintain continued management support as long as the ESS exists. In the beginning, the program will be new and exciting and garnering management support may not be too difficult. As the program grows and matures over time, management support must be continually monitored and enthusiasm rekindled. During difficult economic times, the usefulness of every program will be questioned; it is vital to the long-term effectiveness of the ESS to have unwavering, ongoing executive-level support.

Selecting the Steering Committee

The steering committee for your ESS will be responsible for overseeing the design, development and approval of the proposed suggestion program, in cooperation with the system administrator.

This group will

- Meet periodically (monthly or quarterly is recommended) to refine the rules and procedures of the program

- Be responsible for the final review and approval of ideas submitted to the program

- Get feedback on the implementation and performance of ideas

- Receive reports on the performance of the suggestion program

Steering committee members should represent the major functional areas of the organization (marketing, accounting, finance, purchasing, production, operations, customer service, maintenance, and so on). Select representatives from various levels of the organization, from front-line employees through middle managers and executive vice presidents. If possible, try to balance the committee in terms of geographic representation and in other ways relevant to your particular company. The goal is for the committee to represent a cross section of the different interests, concerns, and skills within the organization. Departments or groups of employees that feel left out will be reluctant to participate in the system.

The committee members should

- have positive attitudes

- look for ways to make the submitted ideas work for the organization

- welcome change and be comfortable with making improvements

- be able to make decisions in a timely manner

- be willing to take chances to improve the organization

Ideally, the number of committee members should be kept between five and nine. Too small a group probably will not represent a broad enough cross section of the organization. Too large a group makes the decision-making process cumbersome and the meetings difficult to manage.

GAINING THE SUPPORT OF EXECUTIVE MANAGEMENT (continued)

Choosing the System Administrator

Obviously a critical element to the success of the ESS, the system administrator is responsible for its day-to-day operation. The administrator reports to the steering committee and conducts the periodic committee meetings. Except in very small organizations, the role of system administrator should be a full-time position.

Who makes a successful administrator? Clearly, the ideal candidate should be positive and enthusiastic about the program, and someone who wants the job. You will want someone who demonstrates leadership qualities and is somewhat familiar with the inner workings of the company. The system administrator should have the following abilities and characteristics. Use these criteria as a checklist when assessing people for the administrator position.

- ☐ Be persuasive, diplomatic, creative and open-minded

- ☐ Adapt under pressure

- ☐ Champion and encourage other people's ideas

- ☐ Work across departmental lines and with all levels of employees

- ☐ Train employees about the ESS

- ☐ Give presentations to everyone

- ☐ Promote the ESS

- ☐ Communicate effectively (written and oral)

- ☐ Analyze data and make decisions

- ☐ Follow through and facilitate the implementation of approved ideas

- ☐ Work with other organizations in exchange programs

STEP 2: DETERMINE GOALS AND OBJECTIVES

The steering committee and the system administrator should determine the primary goals and initial objectives of the ESS before it is launched. The goals will determine the overall thrust and direction of the ESS, and the specific objectives will provide focus for idea generation, promotional efforts and managerial control.

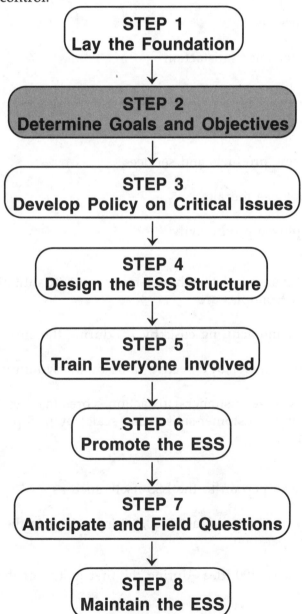

STEP 1
Lay the Foundation

STEP 2
Determine Goals and Objectives

STEP 3
Develop Policy on Critical Issues

STEP 4
Design the ESS Structure

STEP 5
Train Everyone Involved

STEP 6
Promote the ESS

STEP 7
Anticipate and Field Questions

STEP 8
Maintain the ESS

DEFINING YOUR GOALS AND OBJECTIVES

Goals for the system are the long-term aim of the ESS, for example:

- ☑ Reduce costs
- ☑ Increase revenues
- ☑ Refine processes
- ☑ Increase customer satisfaction
- ☑ Reduce waste
- ☑ Improve quality
- ☑ Develop new products and services
- ☑ Boost employee morale
- ☑ Raise employee productivity

Objectives for the system are the shorter-term, more quantitative targets that relate to the goals. Examples are

- ☑ Cut total manufacturing costs by 7% during the current fiscal year.
- ☑ Reduce the number of defective units by 8% within nine months.
- ☑ Increase average customer-satisfaction scores (as measured by the company's customer-satisfaction scale) by 0.25 points within 18 months.

Objectives might also pertain to the ESS itself, such as

- ☑ Justifiably attribute at least $100,000 in savings to the first year of the ESS's operation.
- ☑ Collect at least 100 ideas during the first month of the ESS.

☑ Implement at least 25 ideas during the first four months.

☑ Collect at least one idea from 50% of the employees (or departments) within the first 12 months.

☑ Conduct at least five employee-training sessions during the first 12 months.

☑ For at least 80% of the ideas submitted, reach a decision (to adopt or not to adopt) within at least 40 days.

Important Questions to Consider

Of course, the appropriateness of specific goals and objectives will vary among organizations. However, it's a good idea not to be overly ambitious in the initial goal/objective-setting process. Instead, think in terms of making the ESS an early success, thereby ensuring continued support for the program from both employees and management. Meet modest, attainable objectives first. Then you can proceed to more difficult ones as the organization builds its experience with the ESS.

DEFINING YOUR GOALS AND OBJECTIVES (continued)

Here are a few questions that will help you determine which goals and objectives might reap the largest, earliest successes in your organization.

► *How do your company's performance indicators compare to those of similar-size companies in the industry?*

Consider cost of goods sold, value added (as a percent of sales), profit margin per unit, labor costs (as a percent of total expenses and as a percent of revenues), and the like. Indicators that are out of line may be helped with ideas from an ESS.

► *In what company areas are latent ideas most likely found?*

For example, employee surveys and other feedback mechanisms often reveal highly relevant clues in some departments or functional areas. Employees may believe communication with supervisors is poor, that supervisors do not trust workers, that employee morale is low, that work procedures and standards are too rigid, and so on. These departments or areas may be the most fertile source for improvement ideas. Look at areas where productivity is too low in some functional areas. The most improvement ideas may surface in these departments if employees are encouraged to participate in the ESS.

► *What kinds of improvement ideas potentially involve the most employees?*

For example, almost everyone can be invested in reducing wasted materials or wasted time, but only a limited number of employees may be involved with improving customer service.

► *What would be the profit impact of a ＿＿% improvement in ＿＿?*

Play with alternative scenarios for this. Use 2%, 5%, 10%, and so forth in the first blank, and try out a wide range of improvement possibilities—such as manufacturing costs, paperwork, mailing expenses and number of defects. The answers imply potential priorities for goals and objectives.

In addition to developing goals and objectives for the ESS's internal use and for management's scrutiny, it is also appropriate to prepare a statement of goals for employees' use. This statement need not be detailed, but it should convey to employees what the ESS is all about. An example follows.

ESS Goals Statement

The primary goals of the ESS are to reduce costs, increase productivity and enhance product/service quality by giving employees a chance to share their improvement ideas with the Corporation. This benefits the company, its employees, customers and shareholders.

The Corporation recognizes that employees are in a unique position to identify opportunities for the Corporation to excel. Nobody knows how to improve a job or task better than the person who does it all day.

Although participation in the ESS is voluntary, the Corporation will provide award incentives to employees, with the goal of enlisting every employee in the search for ways to reduce costs, increase productivity, and enhance product/service quality.

STEP 3: DEVELOP POLICY ON CRITICAL ISSUES

The 12 issues described next must be addressed by the committee and the system administrator when making the rules and policies for the ESS. Although other issues may be identified these are critical to the success of the suggestion program.

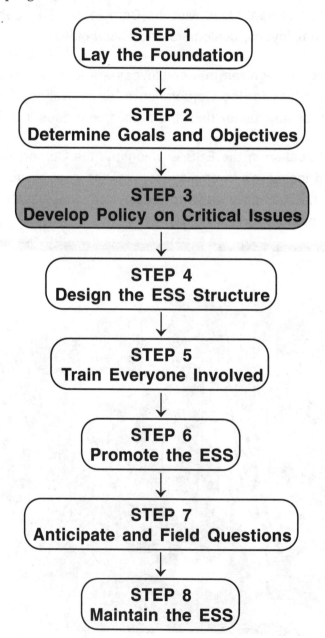

ADDRESSING THE 12 KEY ISSUES

There are at least 12 critical issues that must be addressed initially when making rules and policies.

#1. Eligible Employees

The committee must determine which employees will be eligible to receive awards for their ideas. Some organizations allow everyone on the payroll to participate; others allow only hourly workers or nonmanagement employees to participate. The reason for excluding some people is that innovation, improvement of practices, cost control, and other ESS goals are too central to some workers' primary job responsibilities to allow them to receive additional rewards. Similarly, in many instances, managers may already receive bonuses and rewards for meeting performance goals, so it would be redundant to include them under the ESS umbrella.

In deciding on which groups of workers, staff personnel, supervisors and managers will be eligible, remember that it is easier to incorporate additional groups in the program than it is to exclude groups already participating. This decision must be carefully considered.

#2. Eligible Ideas

The committee must decide what types of ideas will be eligible. Generally, all improvement ideas are eligible except in the following areas.

▶ *Ideas about other employees' compensation and benefits.*

For example, suggestions that the company save money by slashing pay, perks or bonuses of other employees would not be acceptable. One of the attractive by-products of the ESS is that the system can encourage employees to work together to identify and fine-tune ideas. It's necessary to make some suggestions, such as those in the area of compensation and benefits, "off limits." Otherwise, employee in-fighting and interdepartmental conflicts may result.

ADDRESSING THE 12 KEY ISSUES
(continued)

▶ *Suggestions to return to prescribed policies and procedures.*

Ineligible ideas should include those merely reminding management that established policies and procedures have been neglected. For example, if the oil in the company truck is supposed to be changed every 3,000 miles but the maintenance department has been lax in doing so, it's inappropriate to reward an employee for pointing out that maintenance policies aren't being honored. An exception to this guideline would be when an employee can show that there is an error in the operating manual or that a procedure can be simplified without harming the equipment or facilities. For example, someone might recommend that a longer-lasting, synthetic oil be used in the company truck.

▶ *Ideas about conditions of employment.*

Examples are suggestions that only college graduates be hired, or that all workers in the department be capable of lifting 50 pounds. Contact your company's legal staff to make sure the ESS is in compliance with the National Labor Relations Act—especially if the workforce is unionized.

#3. Employee Job Scope

Decide whether suggestions that are within the employee's job scope are acceptable. Some organizations require that a suggestion must be outside the normal scope of an employee's job; other organizations will accept improvement ideas regardless of that criteria.

It is important to remember that most suggestions will be job related but not necessarily within the employee's job scope. The following two questions will help determine job scope:

• Is this the type of suggestion expected from this employee on a regular basis?

• Is this employee paid to do a job in a particular way, or are they paid to make improvements?

#4. Type of Awards

Employees can be rewarded in many ways for their good ideas. Without some form of tangible, valued recognition, however, the ESS is likely to fail. Following are a few options.

► *CASH*

Cash is very popular among employees, but it is more expensive for the company than the other options listed in this section. For clearly quantitative ideas, the company should decide the amount of award (perhaps a specified percentage of the idea's estimated annual net savings), as well as applicability or exclusion of taxes and other payroll deductions. For good ideas that are not as easily quantified, such as those that improve safety or employee morale, a flat amount may be awarded. As a general rule, however, the size of the reward should be related to the magnitude or the net worth of the improvement.

► *MERCHANDISE*

Standard merchandise items—furniture, appliances, television sets and so on—can be awarded to employees with good ideas, or "points" can be accumulated and redeemed for rewards from a company list or catalogue. The latter option encourages employees to continue searching for improvement ideas that will merit additional points.

In either case, merchandise has a high degree of "trophy value." Employees are likely to talk about and show off merchandise they've won—perhaps more so than cash—thereby promoting the ESS. Employees are also more likely to be reminded of their idea each time they use the item, which subtly encourages them to identify additional ideas. Another advantage of merchandise awards is that companies may be eligible for substantial discounts on quantity purchases—discounts employees would not receive if they used cash rewards to purchase similar items.

► *PAID TIME OFF*

A substantial number of full-time employees would gladly exchange a day's wages for an occasional extra day off. Understandably, then, *paid* time off typically is even more highly valued by workers. With some creative scheduling during off-season or lull periods, the company's net loss for granting time off can be nominal.

ADDRESSING THE 12 KEY ISSUES
(continued)

► *LUNCH WITH THE CEO*

This can be a real morale booster for employees, and a perfect opportunity to regularly heighten the CEO's awareness of the ESS.

► *TRAVEL*

Everyone would like to "get away" from time to time, but many people don't because they can't afford it or because they need to spend the money on real-life necessities such as the kids' dental braces or college tuition. With a travel award, employees can take time away and enjoy themselves without feeling guilty. They are also likely to share their pleasant travel memories with coworkers, who may then work harder toward a similar prize.

► *PLAQUES AND CERTIFICATES*

Like merchandise, commemorative plaques and certificates have high trophy and reminder value. For the company, these gifts are relatively low in cost and make for a nice presentation at a company banquet or award luncheon. They also may be granted in conjunction with cash or other awards.

#5. Maximum Award

Maximum awards can range from $500 to $50,000 or more. It is a good idea to pick an amount large enough to encourage the participation of the majority of employees. Don't set the maximum award too low to be attractive. Make the maximum award per idea, not per employee.

#6. Award Distribution

The organization must determine when and how awards will be paid. Options include the following:

When?

- Upon adoption of suggestion

- Upon implementation of suggestion

- After performance of suggestion is proven

How?

- Full award in one lump sum

- A percent paid at adoption of suggestion, with balance paid at implementation

- A percent paid at implementation, and balance paid after benefits are proven

There are many different ways to pay awards, but it is important to pay at least a percentage of the award upon adoption of the suggestion. This shows the employee that the organization values suggestions and that rewards will be promptly given. The balance can be paid later.

#7. Evaluation Process

After ideas are submitted to the ESS office, at least two general approaches may be used to evaluate them.

One option is to have one or more teams of employees evaluate the suggestions. One team might be a manufacturing group, another might be a collection of clerical workers, and so on. Each team evaluates ideas that fall within its realm of expertise.

You can also route each suggestion to one or more appropriate people in the organization for independent evaluations. Each suggestion may travel a different route depending on who can best conduct the evaluation. This approach tends to require greater tracking capabilities than the team evaluation method.

ADDRESSING THE 12 KEY ISSUES
(continued)

#8. Award for Nontraceable Labor Hours Saved

Many suggestions will reduce the number of labor hours needed to do a job, but without decreasing overtime expenditure or number of employees. If the saved hours (or other benefits or savings) are nontraceable, it is a good idea to pay a flat award on the idea and not a percent of the savings.

#9. Tangible vs. Intangible Ideas

Many suggestions will have tangible results that are easy to measure. Others will result in a benefit to the organization that is abstract and difficult to quantify. Safety improvements, ideas to boost employee morale, or ways to improve customer service are typical examples. Rather than trying to base the award on savings or other benefits that are intangible, consider a flat award amount. This will reduce conflicts that otherwise might arise as to the value of a particular idea.

#10. Team Suggestions

In most instances, team suggestions are highly desirable, although the teams should be informal. Suggestions are often more insightful, more creative, and more feasible when more than one person has contributed to them. In addition, consideration of team suggestions encourages employees to share their ideas on their own time (during lunch and breaks), talk up the ESS, and acclimate newer employees to the system.

When the group's idea is first submitted, all team members should sign the submission form. Then, ideally, if a team suggestion is adopted and an award is paid, each team member should receive an equal portion of the award. Keep in mind that cash and merchandise points are more easily distributed in this way than are awards such as travel and merchandise.

#11. Degree of Disclosure

You must decide if suggesters will be allowed to remain anonymous. They may want to if they think this means their suggestion will receive a more objective evaluation. The problem with a suggestion system that allows anonymity is that all communications and clarifications must be routed through the system administrator. This can be cumbersome, and may result in suggestions not being implemented because of communication problems. It is usually more practical to identify the suggester confidentially to the evaluator, so that he or she can follow up directly when clarification or further explanation is needed.

#12. Appeals Procedures

Finally, consideration must be given to employees who believe their unadopted suggestions have not received fair evaluations. One alternative is to allow employees to resubmit their ideas within one year of the original submission, with additional documentation or explanation as necessary. This gives each employee "ownership" of the idea for at least one year.

The ESS office can be instrumental in helping employees fine-tune or document their suggestions, to increase the odds of the ideas being adopted. For example, before accepting a resubmitted idea, the system administrator or his/her representative can meet with the suggester individually to clarify the basis for the evaluation and why the decision not to adopt it was made. For highly technical ideas, it may be necessary to arrange a face-to-face meeting between the suggester, the evaluator and the system administrator.

It is also helpful to grant the system administrator the latitude to decide whether to reconsider a suggestion and, if so, whether to forward it to the same evaluator (or team) or to a different one for a fresh evaluation.

Note: The intent of the ESS is to encourage employees to submit ideas—not discourage them. Never use words and phrases with negative connotations, such as *reject, trash, unsatisfactory,* or *bad idea.*

STEP 4: DESIGN THE ESS STRUCTURE

The structural design phase consists of several substeps: identifying a name and logo for the ESS, designing a process flowchart, articulating rules and eligibility, assembling a policy manual, and designing forms and tracking systems.

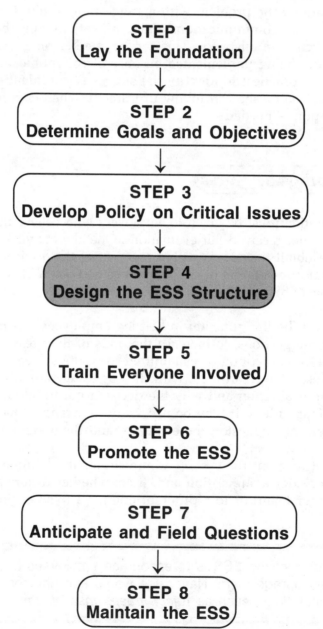

FORMING A PROGRAM IDENTITY

To get the program off to the best possible start, it is important to develop an identity for your ESS. When the program is up and running, and is easily identifiable as its own separate entity, employee buy-in is maximized.

Develop Program Identity

The name of the suggestion program is important. It should remind employees of the program and create a sense of excitement. You don't want to call the program by its generic name (Employee Suggestion System, or ESS). Instead, dub your organization's system with a name that is memorable, reflects some aspect of your organization and conveys the notion of ideas or innovation.

Avoid names that sound overly technical or bureaucratic. For instance, "Employee-Driven Idea System" may sound impressive, but it may be intimidating or unfriendly to rank-and-file employees. These are the people you want to feel comfortable accessing the system, not afraid of it.

Also, watch out for names that may prove to be overly restrictive in the future, should the ESS expand beyond its initial objectives. If the name contains words like "Quality" or "Cost Containment," but the ESS embraces objectives that extend beyond quality and cost containment, then the system's identity may become unclear.

Here are some good examples of ESS names:

- A bank named its suggestion system the "Idea Bank"

- At a hospital, it was "Bright Ideas"

- An airline chose "Ideas in Action"

Design a System Logo

The ESS should have a logo of its own that is distinctive from other programs or departments in the organization. Like the name of the system, the logo should convey something about ideas or innovation. It should be eye catching and should be used on all forms, posters and communications from the ESS office. To ensure that the logo becomes popular and recognizable, design one that represents some aspect of your organization, and have a professional prepare the final artwork. A few sample logos are shown on the next page.

FORMING A PROGRAM IDENTITY
(continued)

ESS logo for a construction company:

ESS logo for a bank:

DESIGNING A PROCESS FLOWCHART

The flowchart of system processes should illustrate step-by-step what happens to a suggestion—from the time it is generated by the employee to the time it is adopted or not adopted and an award or nonadoption letter is sent. Copies of the flowchart should be made available throughout the organization.

Like any flowchart, the design process flowchart is a useful tool for visually communicating the suggestion evaluation process to everyone. It is particularly helpful to show the flowchart to employees who otherwise might expect immediate evaluation and turnaround of their suggestions. The chart is also useful in tracking and controlling the status of ideas as they work through the system. You can use it for diagnosing the current system, with an eye toward improving the process by eliminating, combining or accelerating particular steps.

The example of a process flowchart shown on page 44 illustrates the following elements:

☐ How suggestions are generated

☐ How suggestions are processed

☐ What forms are used

☐ Where forms are sent

☐ How suggestions are recorded

☐ Who evaluates the suggestions

☐ Who makes decisions on suggestions

☐ Who communicates final decisions to suggesters

Of course, this sample flowchart should be modified to fit your organization's specific needs. As an extra control device, the ESS office's copy of the flowchart might be more detailed. For example, it might include the targeted number of days to accomplish each step, with follow-up noted when these deadlines are not met.

DESIGNING A PROCESS FLOWCHART
(continued)

Employee Suggestion Plan System Flowchart

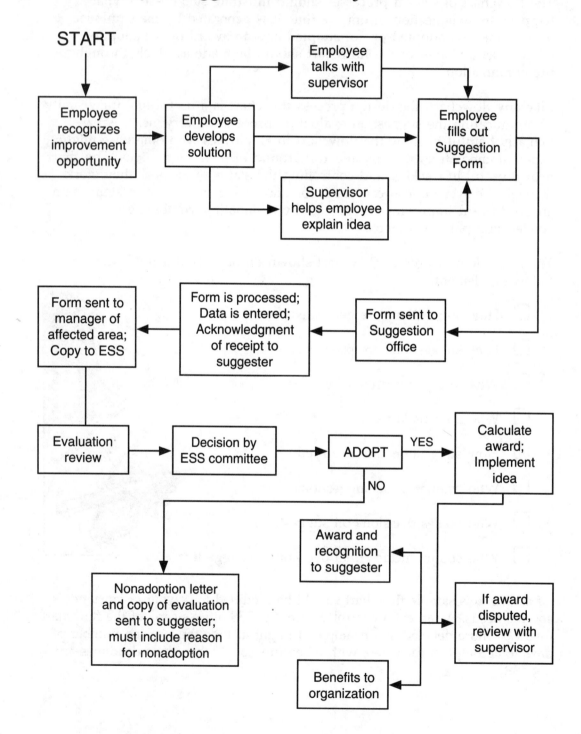

SAMPLE: PROCEDURES FOR USE BY ESS OFFICE

To complement the design process flowchart, a detailed checklist of procedures should be developed as well. Such a checklist is particularly helpful when an ESS has a large volume of ideas in the system. It can record the extended time period they may be at each step and the number of ESS personnel who participate in the processing. Following is a sample checklist of procedures.

- ☐ Receive Suggestion Form in ESS office.

- ☐ Record date of receipt on Suggestion Form.

- ☐ Stamp form with a unique Idea Number.

- ☐ Verify that form is filled out completely and signed by all suggesters.

- ☐ Input idea and suggester information into computer (specifically developed ESS software is available).

- ☐ Record idea in Idea Tracking Log that contains the following:

  - Date received

  - Idea number

  - Receipt sent to suggester

  - Suggestion sent to evaluator

  - Adopted

  - Nonadopted

  - Date closed

  - Suggester notified of decision

  - Suggester name and phone number

  - Evaluator name and phone number

  - Processing turnaround time (number of days)

  - Award amount

SAMPLE (continued)

☐ Make two copies of Suggestion Form and keep the original on file with the ESS administrator.

☐ Send one copy of Suggestion Form and a receipt to the suggester.

☐ Identify proper evaluators for the suggestion.

☐ Send second copy of Suggestion Form and an Evaluation Form to evaluator(s). Record this action in the Idea Tracking Log by checking the appropriate column and listing the name of the evaluator.

☐ Receive Evaluation Form back from evaluator.

☐ Verify that Evaluation Form is completed and signed by all evaluators.

☐ If adoption recommended, notify suggester and calculate reward:

- Calculate award amount

- If estimated savings are over $5,000, have committee review the suggestion

- Notify suggester

- Notify Human Resources to process payment

- File Evaluation Form in "Adopted" file

- Mark the appropriate columns in the Idea Tracking Log

☐ If nonadoption recommended:

- Notify suggester, and include reason for nonadoption

- Answer any questions from the suggester

- File Evaluation Form in "Nonadopt" file

- Mark the appropriate columns in the Idea Tracking Log

ESTABLISHING RULES

As part of the ESS policy determined in Step #3 of building the ESS, specific rules should be developed and articulated. Work closely with your organization's legal counsel when formulating these rules.

This section contains a list of sample rules for the XYZ Corporation. Your company's own version should be printed on the reverse side of the Employee Suggestion Form (discussed later).

There are at least six basic rule categories to address. You'll also need a brief Statement of Control and any other rules that might be needed to customize the ESS for your organization.

(Rule 1) Eligible Participants

Which employees/groups of employees are eligible to participate? Which groups are not eligible?

(Rule 2) Ideas (In)Eligible for Consideration

What types of ideas does the organization want or not want? This section also should describe the submittal process for an idea.

(Rule 3) Duplicate Ideas

How will duplicate ideas be handled? Typically, the first idea received in the suggestion office is eligible for an award. Any duplicate ideas received afterward will not be eligible.

(Rule 4) Team Suggestions

Will the ESS accept ideas submitted jointly? If so, how will they be handled in terms of division of awards, etc.?

ESTABLISHING RULES (continued)

(Rule 5) Awards for Adopted Ideas

The amount of awards and how awards will be distributed.

(Rule 6) Procedure for Unadopted Ideas

How will unadopted ideas be handled? What are the appeal procedures?

Other rules, as determined by Steering Committee and System Administrator

_____

_____

_____

_____

_____

_____

SAMPLE: ESS RULES FOR XYZ CORPORATION

Eligible Participants

Any question of eligibility for an employee to participate in the Employee Suggestion System (ESS) will be decided by the ESS Steering Committee and Administrator. All employees of XYZ Corporation and its subsidiaries are eligible to submit ideas, but only the suggestions of employees outside the management group level are eligible for cash awards. If an employee is eligible at the time a suggestion is submitted, and is then promoted to the management group level prior to the award payment, he or she is still eligible for an award.

Suggestions may be submitted by fax, office mail or hand delivery.

Ideas Eligible for Consideration

► An idea must meet all the requirements to be eligible for an award. Ideas not meeting all requirements will be returned to the suggester.

► All ideas must be submitted on an official Suggestion Form. The Suggestion Form must be completed and signed by the suggester. If a suggestion is cosubmitted by two or more employees, all cosubmitters must sign.

► Eligible ideas must be fully described in writing and explain the estimated reduction in costs, increase in productivity or increased quality of service.

► Eligible ideas must identify the specific problem, and the specific solution to that problem which, when implemented, would result in measurable improvement.

SAMPLE: ESS RULES FOR XYZ CORPORATION (continued)

Ideas Not Eligible for Awards

► Ideas that are not described completely or do not provide a solution to the problem stated.

► Ideas suggesting that current policies or procedures be followed.

► Ideas involving routine maintenance, repairs, housekeeping or normal equipment replacement.

► Ideas that simply voice a complaint. Suggestions should be solution oriented.

► Ideas that result from management's direction to specifically study and resolve an issue.

► An unadopted idea; this includes ideas that are not feasible because of capital budget constraints.

► An idea already under review or in use by XYZ Corporation.

► Ideas dealing with compensation, employee benefits or conditions of employment.

Duplicate Ideas

In the case of duplicate ideas, or ideas that are deemed by XYZ Corporation to be sufficiently similar as to constitute duplicate ideas, the idea stamped in the ESS office with the earliest time and date is eligible for consideration. If two or more duplicate ideas are stamped at the same time, any cash award will be equally divided among the suggesters. The decision of the ESS committee as to whether ideas are duplicates shall be final.

Team Suggestions

Suggestions may be submitted by individuals or by a team. If a team submits an idea, the team must follow these rules:

1. If two or more employees collaborate on an idea, they must submit the idea on one Suggestion Form and identify all collaborators in the space provided on the form.

2. All collaborators must sign the Suggestion Form.

3. If a team's idea is implemented, the award will be shared equally among the collaborators.

Awards for Adopted Ideas

When an idea results in measurable savings to the XYZ Corporation, the award will be equal to 10% of the first year's net savings minus required withholding taxes. The total award amount will not be less than $25 and will not exceed $10,000. The first year's net savings are hard dollar savings estimated over the first 12-month period after implementation of the suggestion minus implementation costs. Ideas that have intangible benefits also may be eligible.

Supervisors of an employee receiving an award will receive an additional award. Supervisor awards will be in the amount of 10% of the amount of the employee award. For example: If an employee receives a $10,000 award, the immediate supervisor will receive an additional $1,000, and that supervisor's manager will receive an additional $1,000. Supervisors are not eligible for an additional award if they are part of a team suggestion.

SAMPLE: ESS RULES FOR XYZ CORPORATION (continued)

Procedure for Unadopted Ideas

► If an idea is determined to be infeasible, the employee may resubmit the idea within one year from the date of the nonadoption correspondence. The idea must be refiled on an official Suggestion Form, and the original Idea Number must be put on the form.

► The decision to forward a resubmitted, unadopted idea is within the sole discretion of the ESS Administrator.

Statement of Control

Once submitted, your idea and accompanying attachments become the property of XYZ Corporation. Decisions on if and how to use the idea, award eligibility and award amount shall be at the complete discretion of the Corporation. All time spent working on ideas outside your normal work schedule is considered voluntary unpaid time, unless otherwise expressly approved in advance by your manager. The Corporation has the exclusive authority to determine policies and procedures and reserves the right to terminate, amend or modify the ESS at any time. Any situation not covered by the rules will be considered by the ESS Steering Committee on a case-by-case basis. Decisions by the ESS Steering Committee shall be final.

WRITING A POLICY MANUAL

It is a good idea to have a policy manual that outlines the policies and procedures of the suggestion program. Copies of the policy manual should be given to managers to assist them in answering questions and otherwise working with employees to increase the number of feasible ideas generated by each department.

Additional copies of the policy manual should be available to employees and evaluators. The policy manual can assist employees by describing techniques for successfully generating ideas, and by outlining the procedures for submitting their suggestions. For evaluators, the manual can include tips for evaluating suggestions and completing the necessary paperwork.

The figure on page 54 is a recommended table of contents for an ESS policy manual. Use it as a checklist and guide to create your own policy manual. Of course, you may want to revise some sections or add additional ones to customize the manual for your organization.

Design Awards Checklist and Worksheet

The sample checklist and worksheet on page 55 may be used to calculate cash awards and track their approval and payment. A well-designed . worksheet reduces the likelihood of errors, improves system control and may be referred to if future questions about the award arise.

SAMPLE AHEAD . . .

SAMPLE: ESS POLICY MANUAL
TABLE OF CONTENTS

XYZ Corporation

Table of Contents

ESS Objectives

System Flowchart

Eligible Participants

Ideas Not Eligible for Awards

Duplicate Ideas

Team Suggestions

Awards for Adopted Ideas

Cash Awards Checklist (see sample on the next page)

Procedure for Resubmitting Unadopted Ideas

Statement of Control

How to Submit an Idea

Tips for Suggesters
  Your ideas are valuable!
  Benefits to you!
  Why ask employees for ideas?

How to Develop Your Suggestion

How to Submit a Suggestion

Questions to Stimulate Ideas

Tips for Evaluators: What Is Your Role?

Evaluation Checklist

Evaluator Things to Do

Sample Forms

Rules

Cash Awards Checklist and Worksheet for Idea # _____

☐ Savings amount calculated by evaluator $ _____

☐ Total award amount calculated by ESS administrator:

Hard dollar savings for first 12 months
after implementation $ _____

Less: Implementation costs

_____ _____

_____ _____

_____ _____

_____ _____ −$ _____

Net savings (year 1)   _____

×: Award percentage   _____ %

Award amount* (includes applicable taxes
and other payroll deductions) $ _____

☐ Reasons for significant differences between evaluator's estimate of
savings and ESS administrator's estimate (if applicable):

_____

_____

_____

☐ Savings verified and approved by committee   _____

☐ Award amount verified and approved by committee _____

_____ Date approved

☐ Amount to be awarded at implementation   _____

_____ Date awarded by Human Resources

_____ or other (specify)

☐ Amount to be awarded after test period

_____ Date awarded by Human Resources

_____ or other (specify)

*Maximum award amount $ _____ ; minimum award $ _____ ; flat
amount for nonquantifiable ideas $ _____

DESIGN AN EMPLOYEE SUGGESTION FORM

The Employee Suggestion Form is used to document the suggester's idea. It also will be used in the tracking and evaluation process. The form should contain the following eight sections. A sample Employee Suggestion Form is provided on page 101.

Tracking Information

This section includes information that will allow the ESS office to keep track of the suggestion. A copy of a sample form is included on page 101. It includes the following:

- Time/date received

- Suggestion number

- Keywords used to file

- Evaluator name

How to Fill Out the Form

At a minimum, this section should instruct suggesters to (a) Type or print when completing the form; (b) Attach additional pages if needed; (c) Complete all sections, including signing and dating the form (all cosuggesters should sign the form); (d) Forward the completed form to the ESS office.

Additional tips or instructions may be included as well. For example:

- Be sure to read the ESS rules (printed on the reverse side of the form). Contact the ESS office for clarification of any rules.

- Consult your supervisor to get help with the idea and to increase its chances of being accepted.

- Describe the PROBLEM as if the evaluator knows nothing about the situation.

- Describe the SOLUTION in detail, attaching supporting documents if necessary.

- Show how the dollar values were calculated. What are the cost components?

- Identify the person and/or departments who should implement the suggestion.

Personal Information on Suggester

This section includes the following:

- Last name, first, middle initial

- Social Security Number

- Phone number

- Department

- Location (City-State)

- Position/Title

Description of Suggestion

This section describes the improvement the employee is suggesting. For some ideas and suggesters, pictures or diagrams may be helpful in communicating the idea.

Description of Current Method

This section describes the current situation that the employee is recommending to change. It provides information to evaluators and committee members who may be unfamiliar with the current methods being used.

DESIGN A SUGGESTION FORM (continued)

Savings or Benefits

This section describes the benefits or savings that the organization will receive from this suggestion. Encourage suggesters to go ahead and submit their ideas even if some of the costs and savings data are unknown or difficult to determine. Rough estimates are better than no estimates.

Signature

This section is provided for the signature of the suggester. All suggesters cosubmitting the idea must sign here. This section should state that the suggesters have read and understood the rules of the program before they sign.

Rules

The rules should be printed on the reverse side of the suggestion form so that each suggester is able to read them before submitting an idea.

DESIGN AN EVALUATION FORM

This form will be used by the evaluator and then reviewed by the ESS administrator to determine if the suggestion is feasible for the organization. The Evaluation Form will also be used to estimate the savings or benefit of the suggestion. This form should be attached to the Employee Suggestion Form so they will remain together throughout the evaluation process.

A sample Idea Evaluation Form is included on page 102. Note that it includes three primary sections:

Evaluator Information

- Evaluator name

- Evaluator phone number

- Department of evaluator

- Evaluator location (city, state)

Summary of Expected Benefits

This section is used by the evaluator to determine whether or not the suggestion should be adopted and implemented. This section also is used to determine the amount of savings or benefits the organization is expected to receive from this suggestion.

Award Recommendation

This section is used by the ESS administrator and the Steering Committee to determine the amount of award for an adopted suggestion.

DEVELOP EMPLOYEE SUGGESTION FORM DISTRIBUTION AND LOCATION LIST

This list should indicate the locations where employees can obtain Suggestion Forms. These forms should be easily accessible to all employees, to encourage regular use. Suggestion Forms may be included in employee handbooks and made available in ESS training and orientation materials. Additional forms should be located in areas where employee traffic is heavy. For example, consider the following locations:

- In break rooms

- Near time-clocks

- In all departments

- Near copy machines

- Near water fountains

- In the Training Center

- In the Human Resources department

- In the ESS office

Design a Tracking System

The tracking system can be manual or it can be computerized. Manual tracking systems are acceptable if the organization is relatively small and the number of suggestions will be small. A sample Tracking Log used in manual systems is included on page 103. If the organization is large, however, or a substantial volume of suggestions is expected, it is probably worth the investment to computerize the suggestion system. There are several computer programs available. Contact the Employee Involvement Association for more information (telephone 703–524–3424).

P A R T

III

Introducing the ESS
to the Organization

STEP 5: TRAIN EVERYONE INVOLVED

With widespread participation and support throughout the organization, the ESS is likely to succeed. Being involved and supportive means understanding the ESS and how everyone can make it a success. Knowledge is not automatic, nor is it fully realized by simply reading the ESS policy manual. Training is required.

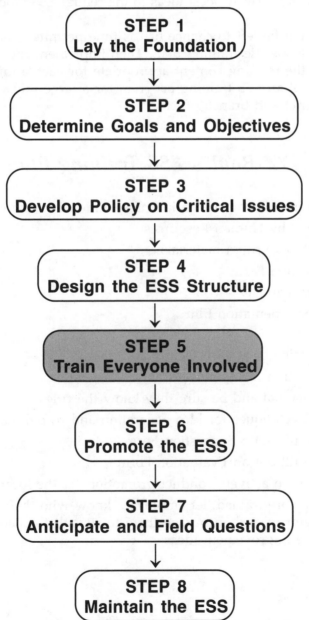

IMPLEMENTING THE TRAINING PLAN

The ESS administrator must work closely with the organization's professional training staff to develop training programs suitable for employees, supervisors, managers, evaluators and the ESS steering committee. Large, geographically dispersed organizations also may wish to develop training programs for local coordinators or advocates who will promote the ESS, assist employees with their suggestions and forward local ideas to the central ESS office.

Training should not be left to chance or "as time permits." Rather, think in terms of having a specific training plan. Then implement the plan—which should consider the training content appropriate for each audience. Following is an outline of an ESS training program for a large midwestern bank with several district and branch offices.

XYZ Bank's ESS Training Plan

I. Design and implement orientation presentation for new employees.
   A. Performed by Human Resources
   B. Will include written materials
      1. Suggestion Form
      2. Policy manual
   C. Show ESS orientation film

II. Train a coordinator at each facility and district
   A. Show the film for employees and managers
   B. Give a manual and be sure they know the rules
   C. Train in techniques for idea generation and recognition
   D. Teach to fill out a Suggestion Form
   E. Teach to fill out an Evaluation Form
   F. Encourage to actively conduct promotions at the local level
   G. Once they are trained, let employees know who their local coordinator is, and encourage them to consult the coordinators when they have improvement ideas

III. Visit each facility and district office and give presentations to all managers and employees
   A. Show manager film
   B. Show employee film
   C. Give every person a Suggestion Form
   D. Review rules with every employee in a group meeting
   E. Review system flowchart
   F. Give inspirational stories and examples of employees who have submitted ideas and received awards

IV. Give presentation to all bank presidents
   A. Show manager film
   B. Give samples
      1. Policy manual
      2. Suggestion Form
      3. Evaluation Form
   C. Offer performance statistics on the ESS
   D. Convince them that if they help get employees to participate, the entire company will benefit greatly
   E. Give them a national perspective on ESSs so they will realize XYZ is not the only company doing this
   F. Give inspirational examples of employees who have received awards
   G. Let them know that we are tracking performance on all districts. Offer monthly updates on their districts if they are interested.

V. Train all people who travel regularly to other facilities and districts.
   A. Give the same training as the facility coordinators.
   B. Give literature to distribute (cards, brochures, etc.)
   C. Point out that these employees can be spokespersons for the ESS and that their efforts in spreading the word are greatly appreciated.
   D. Give strong emphasis to idea spotting and awareness training to these employees. Ask them to encourage people in the offices they visit to submit suggestions and ideas.

IMPLEMENTING THE TRAINING PLAN (continued)

    E. Have them report to the ESS administrator any ideas that they hear about when traveling. They can let the administrator know that someone has an idea. The administrator can then follow-up by contacting the prospective suggesters and helping them with the suggestion submission process.

VI. Design a training class that the training center can teach. Include the following:

    A. Basics of the ESS (procedures and rules)

    B. Idea-generation techniques

    C. Idea-spotting techniques

    D. Solution formulation

    E. Inspirational examples of award recipients

VII. Focus special training on areas of the corporation that have many processes.

    A. Operations departments

    B. Supply areas

    C. Records management

    D. Mail operations

Training Content

A key consideration of the training plan is the content of the training program. As indicated in the sample training plan for XYZ Bank, not everyone in the organization has the same training needs. Employees, for example, will be more interested in ESS rules and idea-generation techniques than will evaluators. Of course, the ESS administrator and office staff should be familiar with each content area. New ESS administrators may wish to contact the Employee Involvement Association (EIA) for additional training (703-524-3424).

Training Content Worksheet

KEY: SC = ESS steering committee
Em = Employees throughout the organization
Ev = Evaluators (team) or prospective evaluators
M = Managers and supervisors throughout the organization

Training Content	Primary Audiences	Secondary Audiences
1. ESS Goals and Objectives	SC, M, Ev	Em
2. Organizational Policy on Critical Issues	SC, M, Em	Ev

• Eligible Employees
  • Eligible Ideas
  • Employee Job Scope
  • Types of Awards
  • Maximum Award
  • Award Distribution
  • Evaluation Process
  • Nontraceable Labor Hours
  • Tangible/Intangible Ideas
  • Team Suggestions
  • Degree of Disclosure
  • Appeals Procedure		

3. Program Rules	SC, M, Em	Ev
4. Employee Motivation Techniques	Em	M
5. Idea Generation and Problem Spotting Techniques	M, Em	
6. Completing the Suggestion Form	Em	M, Ev
7. Promotional Techniques and Programs	M, Em	SC, Ev
8. Evaluation Process	SC, M, Ev	Em
9. Other: _____		
10. Other: _____		
11. Other _____		
12. Other: _____		

SPOTTING PROBLEMS AND GENERATING IDEAS

Beyond introducing the organization to the ESS, a key training objective should be teaching employees and their supervisors specific techniques for idea generation and problem spotting. Even with these techniques, employees still must utilize their own experience, intuition and creativity—but the techniques will help them to be more alert to potential ideas. Ultimately, they will develop more feasible ideas than they might otherwise.

Examples of some of these idea-generation and problem-spotting training exercises are presented on the next few pages.

THREE DOZEN QUESTIONS TO STIMULATE IDEAS

1. How can it be done better?

2. How are others doing it?

3. Can it be eliminated? How?

4. Can we do it better elsewhere? How?

5. Could it be done in a different sequence? How?

6. Could a machine do it? How?

7. Is there a better method? What?

8. Can you eliminate motions? Which ones?

9. Can you make your work easier? How?

10. Can you make your work less tiring? How?

11. Can you eliminate paperwork? How?

12. Can things be put to use that are being discarded? Which ones and how?

13. Can we do two at a time? How?

14. Can we do four or more at a time? How?

15. Can yields be increased? How?

16. Can quality be increased? How?

17. Is there a less-expensive way? What is it?

THREE DOZEN QUESTIONS TO STIMULATE IDEAS (continued)

18. Can a bottleneck be eliminated? How?

19. Can it be done faster? How?

20. Can scrap be eliminated? How?

21. Can any duplication be eliminated? How?

22. Can equipment downtime be eliminated? How?

23. Can lost production time be eliminated? How?

24. Can one person do it as fast as two? How?

25. Can you and a machine do it as fast as two other people? How?

26. Can delays be eliminated? How?

27. Is better equipment available? What is it?

28. Have you tried a group discussion to solve a problem? Can you do that?

29. Can one person run two machines? How?

30. Can the workplace be rearranged to increase productivity? How?

31. Can the work be made more interesting? How?

32. Can idle time be used more productively? How?

33. Can steps in a process be eliminated? How?

34. Can steps in a process be combined? How?

35. Could the task be done by customers, suppliers or someone else, instead of employees? How?

36. Could the job be done by part-time or less-skilled workers rather than by full-time, highly skilled workers? How?

More Ways to Spot Valuable Ideas!

Listen for the following phrases in your office or department. These "trigger" phrases can alert you to listen carefully; they very often are followed by good ideas. They serve to bring your attention to areas that may need improvement.

- *We should have . . .*
- *We could have . . .*
- *We ought to start . . .*
- *I wish we could . . .*
- *I wish we had . . .*
- *We shouldn't have to . . .*
- *Wouldn't it be nice if . . .*
- *If only we had . . .*
- *If only we could . . .*
- *Why didn't we . . .*
- *It would be a lot easier if we . . .*
- *I wish we didn't have to . . .*
- *I hate doing . . .*

- *It is too complicated to . . .*
- *Next time we should . . .*
- *This is too expensive . . .*
- *It seems wasteful to . . .*
- *ABC company does it this way . . .*
- *I can't believe we . . .*
- *What if we . . .*
- *Are you sure we have to . . .*
- *I bet we could . . .*
- *I suggest we . . .*
- *There ought to be a better way to . . .*
- *I've often wondered why we don't . . .*

Learn to pay attention when you hear these phrases and be ready to take action when you spot a good idea. When you hear these phrases or catch yourself using them, take a little time to explore what caused your concern or dislike. You may be close to a good idea or a way to improve something. Once you have formulated your great idea, get an official Employee Suggestion Form and submit your idea to the ESS office. Your idea may qualify you for a substantial award!

STILL MORE WAYS TO GENERATE IDEAS

To get your creativity flowing, consider the following tips.

☐ *Think of ideas that will*

- Eliminate duplication

- Reduce paperwork

- Reduce errors

- Reduce rework

- Reduce the number of steps in a process

- Reduce waste

- Generate new revenue

- Trim costs

- Save time and labor

- Simplify procedures

☐ *Challenge old habits.* Just because you have been doing something a certain way for a long time does not mean that it has to be done that way forever. Analyze everything you do and make sure there is a good reason for doing it.

☐ *Ask your family members and friends.* What do they do at their jobs to reduce costs? People outside your industry may have good ideas that we could adopt.

☐ *Scan magazines, newspapers or catalogs for ideas.* Keep your eyes open for changes that would reduce our costs or improve our quality.

☐ *Think of things you did at places you have worked previously.* Maybe your former employer did things more efficiently than what you have seen here.

☐ *Have a brainstorming party.* Get together with a group of coworkers and make some lists of problems and solutions. Then refine the list to a group of workable ideas.

☐ *Draw a blueprint or flowchart of the work tasks in your department.* In the diagram, show the specific steps done in each task. Who does them? In what sequence? Then examine the diagram and see if you think some steps could be eliminated or combined. Could some steps be speeded up? Could some steps be automated or simplified? How? Is it necessary for so many people to be involved in the process? At which steps do the majority of problems seem to occur, and how might they be eliminated? And so on.

☐ *Visit a competitor's place of business (if accessible to the public).* What do the employees there do that is different from your workplace? Does their arrangement of equipment and physical facilities make a difference? As a customer, what are your impressions of the competitor's customer service and product quality? Can you think of how those methods could be applied (or avoided, if negative) in our company?

TRAINING FOR EVALUATORS

Evaluators represent another critical training audience. Unless they take the system seriously and fill their roles professionally, the success of the ESS will be jeopardized. Here is a brief guide that may be used as a basis for conducting a training program for evaluators and/or distributed as a written reminder and tip sheet for evaluators.

Tips for Evaluators

Congratulations! You have been selected to evaluate an idea suggested by a fellow employee. This tip sheet will assist you in making that evaluation. Your evaluation is a key ingredient in making the ESS work effectively. Here are some useful tips to follow when evaluating suggestions:

 Immediately read the suggestion form and related records, reports and other documentation. If the idea has already been suggested, return it to the ESS.

 Make sure you are the appropriate person to evaluate the idea. You were selected because you have expertise in the subject matter and authority to implement the suggestion if it is adopted.

 Be sure you understand the idea. Contact the suggester personally and discuss the idea if necessary.

 Evaluate the suggestion. Talk to the appropriate people and gather the necessary information to conduct a fair and complete evaluation. Rather than looking for reasons why the idea won't work, look for ways to make it work. Also, consider using the idea on a companywide basis. Evaluate the idea, not the person submitting it; don't let personalities influence your decision.

TIP 5 Prepare a clear, legible evaluation and recommendation on the attached Evaluation Form. Be direct; get to the point. Define acronyms and abbreviations you use. Avoid vague phrases such as "I don't think it will work," or "It is working okay now." Be specific! Keep in mind that the suggester will receive a copy of the evaluation. If you recommend that a suggestion not be adopted, be sure to list specific reasons for your recommendation. If possible, offer information that will help the suggester refine and resubmit the idea.

TIP 6 Be prompt! The evaluation is due in the ESS office within 30 calendar days of your receiving it. If you cannot complete the evaluation within 30 days, contact the ESS office and request an extension. When the evaluation is completed, send the Idea Evaluation Form and the Employee Suggestion Form to the ESS office.

Thank You!

Anyone with a good idea should get
the VIP treatment!

STEP 6: PROMOTE THE ESS

Training introduces the ESS to the organization and teaches everyone the mechanics of their involvement. Promotion, on the other hand, is necessary to motivate participation and continually remind people of the ESS.

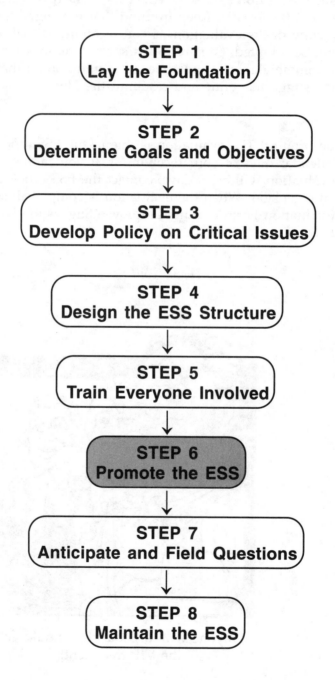

ENSURING SUCCESS

For the ESS to be successful, employees must understand the program and how to generate and submit ideas; this is achieved through training. But they also must be aware of and enthusiastic about the ESS, so they'll make the effort to participate; this is achieved through promotion. Clearly, training and promotion are synergistic. Both are critical components of a successful ESS.

To increase the odds of a successful and coherent promotional effort, a proactive plan is essential. The initial promotion plan should be coordinated with the training plan. It also should reflect three different time frames: Prelaunch, First Year, Special and Intermittent.

Prelaunch Promotions

Before the program officially begins to accept suggestions, a prelaunch promotional effort should be executed to get people interested in what is about to happen—to make them curious. Tell employees to begin looking for improvement ideas and that they could win up to $10,000 (or whatever your company's maximum award is) if their ideas are used. Set up the prelaunch promotion to occur one to two months before the ESS is formally launched.

First Year Promotional Plan

The promotional campaign should be planned a year in advance. This allows adequate time to make arrangements and design and produce promotional material. Within the first few weeks or months, diligently strive for the approval of a "Big One" (idea and award) and greatly publicize it. A variety of promotional tools and outlets may be utilized in the context of several promotional objectives, as outlined below.

▶ *To remind employees of the ESS, and to prompt ideas:*

☐ Posters

☐ Flyers

☐ Table tents

☐ Paycheck stickers and stuffers (see example on page 80)

ENSURING SUCCESS (continued)

► *To demonstrate the organization's commitment to the ESS:*

☐ Articles in company bulletins

☐ Videos

☐ Ask company executives to talk about the ESS in their speeches

☐ Encourage supervisors to make regular references to the ESS in departmental meetings

► *To inspire and motivate employees to submit ideas:*

☐ Articles in company bulletins

☐ Award ceremonies

☐ Publicize the winning employees and winning ideas in company bulletins

☐ ESS videos

► *To recognize employees, supervisors, evaluators, implementers and others involved in the success of the ESS:*

☐ Award ceremonies and recognition banquets

☐ Photo sessions with company executives

☐ Pictures and articles in bulletins and other corporate communications

☐ Involve Public Relations department in generating external publicity

☐ Thank-you notes and letters

► *To provide detailed information, answer specific questions and assist employees in refining their ideas:*

☐ Have the ESS administrator and staff personally meet and interact with as many employees as possible

☐ Make as many ESS presentations at the departmental level as possible

☐ Maintain an open-door policy to informally chat with employees

☐ Include the location and/or phone number of the ESS office on all promotional material

☐ Videos regarding the ESS

► *Consider other promotional vehicles readily available in your organization, or identify additional ones needed to customize your company's ESS:*

_____

_____

_____

_____

_____

EFFECTIVE LISTENING → ← EFFECTIVE RESPONSE

SAMPLE: PAYCHECK STUFFER . . .

Do You Have an Idea?
Tips for ESS Suggesters

(Your Ideas Are Valuable!)

If you have a good idea that will reduce costs, generate new revenue or result in higher-quality products for our customers, then we want that idea. When the savings are measurable, we are willing to pay you up to $10,000 for it. The ESS was designed to give employees like you a chance to share your good ideas. When ideas are shared, the employees, Corporation, stockholders and customers all benefit. For details, see the official ESS rules printed on the back of the Employee Suggestion Form.

(Benefits to You)

A suggestion can provide you with the following benefits:

- Cash awards for adopted and implemented suggestions
- Recognition for individual achievement
- Personal satisfaction knowing you contributed
- Opportunity to see your ideas in actual use

(Why Ask You for Ideas?)

- *You* know where the hidden costs are.
- *You* know where duplication and unnecessary delays are.
- *You* know why it's inefficient to continue a current practice.
- *You* know how the customer can be better served.
- *You* know your job and how to improve it better than anyone else.

Share your ideas with the ESS office today!

Special, Intermittent Promotions

It is normal to receive a flood of ideas during the first three months following the launch of a new ESS. If the organization is ripe for potential improvements and the ESS office handles the initial onslaught of ideas promptly, courteously and professionally, the healthy stream of ideas can continue. Eventually, however, you can expect a lull.

Special promotions may be used to offset the eventual and inevitable downturn in suggestions submitted. These may include generic promotional blitzes in which more of the same promotional efforts are put forth. Or, more effectively, they may direct the organization's attention to specific themes that target areas needing improvement. As an example, an intermittent promotion is included on page 82. Here are some other possibilities:

- Postage economy

- Utility bill reduction

- Reports simplification

- Waste cutting

- Rework reduction

- New product/service ideas

- Other: _____

Additional prizes or incentives may be offered during these special theme promotions that might span a six- to eight-week period. Such extra awards may be directed toward the individual or toward the department or division. For example, offer an extra $100 to the department that submits the most adopted ideas. This team approach is a great way to enlarge the pool of employees who participate in the ESS. Workers already familiar with the ESS and who are comfortable submitting ideas are likely to encourage and assist coworkers to get involved, as well.

When activating these special promotions, be sure to communicate a deadline for submissions. Also, point out that other ideas which don't necessarily fit the theme are still welcome during the theme promotion period, as always.

SPECIAL, INTERMITTENT PROMOTIONS (continued)

It's Open Season on Unnecessary Reports! Special ESS Promotion

The ESS has declared OPEN SEASON on unnecessary REPORTS, and the hunting season begins soon. Starting June 1, you can turn those reports that you receive and never use into cash.

Here's how it works . . .

If you receive a report that you don't use and don't need, staple that report to an ESS Suggestion Form. You and your manager sign the form and send it to the ESS office. Each copy of a paper report that is eliminated is worth $10.00. If you convert a paper copy to fiche it is worth $10.00. Reducing the frequency of a report is worth $10.00. Eliminate the generation of an entire report, and you get $100.00!

There will also be a prize drawing at the end of the promotion. Each time you submit a report to be eliminated, your name will be put into a hopper. At the end of the promotion we will draw two names, and those two employees will win $500.00 each. So, submit as many reports as you can and increase your chances of winning the drawing.

This promotion will run from June 1 to July 31, 19XX. The normal rules of the ESS do not apply to this promotion. Every employee of the corporation is eligible to participate. If you have questions about this promotion, call the ESS office.

Of course, the XYZ Corporation has the exclusive authority to determine policies and procedures and reserves the right to terminate, amend or modify this promotion at any time. Awards will be dependent on the actual elimination of the report. There may be incidents in which a report cannot be eliminated.

Note: Ideas not dealing with the elimination of reports will be handled through the ESS as usual.

STEP 7: ANTICIPATE AND FIELD QUESTIONS

With the development and introduction of any new program or system, employees and managers will inevitably raise several questions, concerns and even criticisms. Employee suggestion systems are no different in this respect.

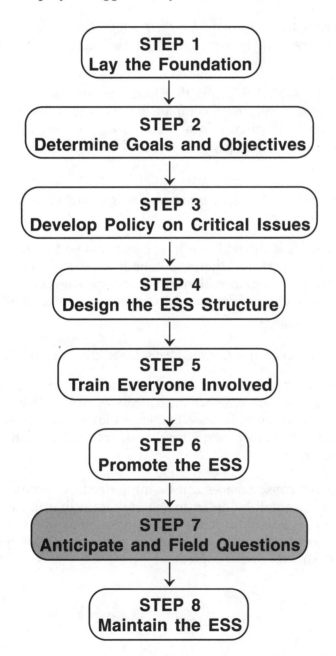

STEP 1
Lay the Foundation

STEP 2
Determine Goals and Objectives

STEP 3
Develop Policy on Critical Issues

STEP 4
Design the ESS Structure

STEP 5
Train Everyone Involved

STEP 6
Promote the ESS

STEP 7
Anticipate and Field Questions

STEP 8
Maintain the ESS

ANSWERING 13 COMMON QUESTIONS

Here is a list of questions you should anticipate, followed by suggested answers. Of course, you'll want to customize your responses based on the ESS crafted in your organization.

Q #1: *If employees are being paid for their suggestions, isn't there a risk that employees will be secretive about their ideas to keep them from being stolen by other employees?*

A: The data generated by firms that have already implemented ESSs suggests otherwise. These companies have found that their employees are *more* likely to discuss ideas with coworkers—especially when employees are encouraged to submit ideas as a team.

Q #2: *Will teamwork suffer because individuals guard their ideas too closely?*

A: Again, there is little evidence to support this sort of fear. Encourage employees to work together and submit ideas asa team. Remind them that by working together, they can fine-tune suggestions and make them more workable, thereby increasing the chance of adoption.

Q #3: *Will morale suffer if one employee's ideas are "stolen" by another?*

A: Occasionally employees who submit similar ideas independently will suspect and question whether their idea was stolen. This problem occurs infrequently, however, because employees know they must continue to work with one another long after the suggestion has been adopted and rewarded.

The negative consequences can be minimized by reminding employees that preference will be given to the idea form that is submitted *first*. In addition, it is helpful if the ESS office is available to explain why one employee's idea was not adopted although a coworker's seemingly similar idea was adopted.

Q #4: *Employees are supposed to look for ways to improve the company's productivity—that's part of their job. Why should we pay extra for that?*

A: Of course, the company has complete discretion as to whether an ESS is implemented, and how much to reward employees for workable ideas. If the company chooses not to develop a program, many employees will volunteer ideas anyway—to their credit and the company's benefit. Historically, however, adopting an ESS has clearly resulted in more ideas that would otherwise have been stifled.

Q #5: *Will morale suffer if an employee's idea is rejected because management is already working on it?*

A: This is an understandable concern. Employees may be discouraged from submitting suggestions if they think that management is "stealing" their ideas. One approach is to keep employees informed about the programs management is already addressing; for instance, you might post the minutes of Executive Committee meetings. Another approach is to carefully explain to employees why their ideas were not adopted.

Q #6: *How should we deal with employees who seem to submit ideas almost daily, most of which are not well developed and not workable?*

A: Some employees may wrongly assume that the winning ideas are selected at random, so they may submit ideas "by the pound." This phenomenon usually subsides after workers see that most of their ideas are not adopted.

It helps to remind people that the selection of ideas is based on merit, not chance. Encourage employees to talk over their ideas with supervisors before formally submitting them. In addition, the system administrator should have some latitude to refuse to forward ideas for evaluation.

ANSWERING 13 COMMON QUESTIONS (continued)

Q #7: *What if the company awards money to an employee for an idea that later proves to be unworkable?*

A: The company should stand behind the adoption decision and honor commitments made to employees. Each adopted idea should be viewed as an investment. Like any investment, suggestions carry with them risks and uncertainty. The investment return will be higher than expected for some suggestions, and lower than expected for others.

Employees who submit their ideas, as well as the ESS office that screens and evaluates them, make recommendations based upon the best information or estimates available at the time. Neither the employees nor the ESS office should be reprimanded or otherwise discouraged. Over time, the precision of estimates should improve.

Q #8: *An ESS sounds very bureaucratic, time-consuming, and expensive to administer. Isn't there an easier way?*

A: The size and the complexity of the ESS is related to the size and the complexity of the company. For very small companies, the suggestion program doesn't need to be as formal as ones for larger, diversified companies. For example, fewer people can be involved in the screening and evaluation process, and ideas can be tracked manually.

However, careful thought should be given to the development and implementation of the ESS—because the potential payoffs are tremendous. In this sense, the ESS should not be viewed as another administrative burden, but as an opportunity to improve productivity, cut costs, increase quality, boost employee morale and enhance customer satisfaction.

Q #9: *Should I be concerned that employees will spend too much time trying to think up new ideas and not enough time doing their jobs?*

A: No. Companies that have already adopted ESSs report few problems in this regard. Employees who actively seek out and critically assess ideas usually do so in the context of their own jobs, while performing their normal day-to-day tasks. Employees typically will discuss and evaluate ideas before and after work, during their lunch period, and when otherwise off the clock.

Q #10: *How should ideas for one-shot programs be handled? For example, suppose we open a new location and get dozens of ideas for improving the expansion process, staging "grand opening" promotions and so on, but because we rarely open new locations the ideas may never pay off?*

A: There are at least two ways to handle this issue. One is to simply declare ideas for such programs to be ineligible. The other is to base the awards on net savings realized within the first year (or another appropriate time period). Thus, if the "one-shot program" is not repeated within the specified time period, there would be no savings and hence no reward.

Q #11: *It seems inevitable that some employees who submit unadopted ideas will disagree with the decision. Should we establish some sort of grievance procedure or allow employees to resubmit their ideas?*

A: Of course, some employees will disagree. However, if the review and evaluation procedure is carefully designed and clearly communicated, employees will be less likely to perceive any deliberate bias or thoughtless action on the part of the ESS office. Another key is to provide thoughtful and—when possible—personalized feedback to employees whose ideas are not adopted. If an employee still feels strongly that an idea did not receive fair evaluations, he or she can be allowed to resubmit the suggestion with additional documentation.

If your company is typical, most suggestions will not be adopted, so it is important to communicate the reasons for the negative decision. This helps maintain employees' interest in submitting ideas and increases the likelihood that their future submissions will be adopted.

Q #12: *The feasibility of many ideas hinges on an understanding of costs. Should cost data be freely shared with employees? Should employees have unlimited access to such data?*

A: This question reinforces the importance of employees working closely with their supervisors. Often supervisors have a firm grasp on cost data and other considerations that would help employees fine-tune their ideas.

ANSWERING 13 COMMON QUESTIONS
(continued)

Moreover, the decision to adopt or not adopt suggestions should not depend on the accuracy of cost estimates. Employees should be encouraged to carefully think through their ideas and gather supporting documentation prior to submission as best they can. For instance, the employee may be aware of a machine, process, tool, alternative ingredient or other element that ESS reviewers may not be familiar with. Submission requirements that are too rigid may discourage employees from offering their ideas.

Q #13: *Will employees hesitate to offer suggestions if they believe the adoption of the idea will put them or their coworkers out of a job?*

A: Possibly. Although most adopted ideas will not have such a dramatic effect, some can—as when technology is introduced to perform tasks previously done manually. To allay these fears, the company should assure workers that although the nature of their jobs may change, and in some cases employees may be transferred to other departments, employees will not be dismissed as a result of the ESS.

PART

IV

Fine-Tuning
the ESS

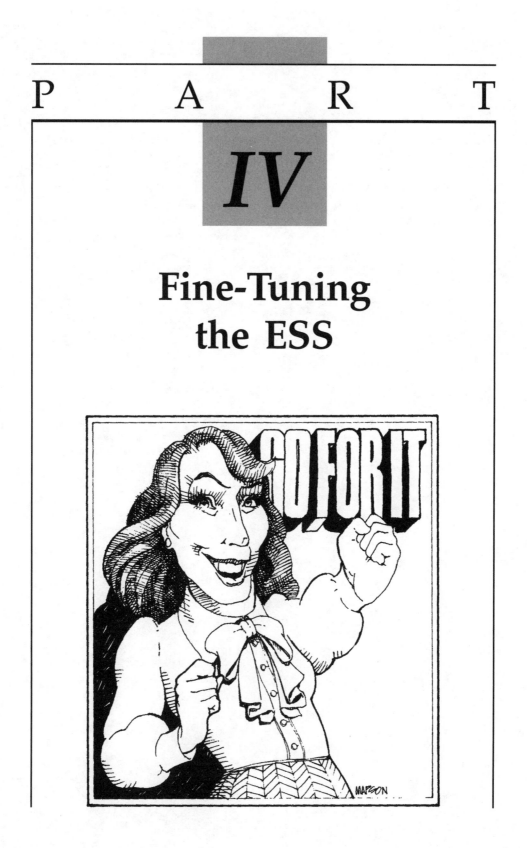

P A R T

IV

Fine-Tuning
the GSP

STEP 8: MAINTAIN THE ESS

A fundamental principle driving the ESS is that everything can be improved, and this principle applies to the ESS, as well. There is always an opportunity to update, expand, clarify, streamline or otherwise improve suggestion programs. By looking at the basic ESS program itself, there is the opportunity to maintain the ESS to ensure that it stays a viable program. Without upkeep and maintenance, the program runs the risk of falling by the wayside.

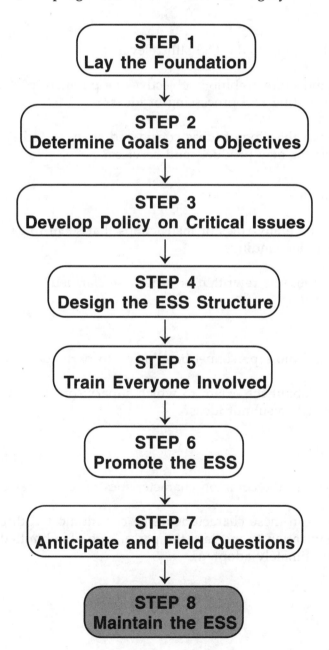

STEP 1
Lay the Foundation

↓

STEP 2
Determine Goals and Objectives

↓

STEP 3
Develop Policy on Critical Issues

↓

STEP 4
Design the ESS Structure

↓

STEP 5
Train Everyone Involved

↓

STEP 6
Promote the ESS

↓

STEP 7
Anticipate and Field Questions

↓

STEP 8
Maintain the ESS

MAINTAINING AND IMPROVING THE ESS

Of course, suggestions from employees should be welcomed and encouraged. In addition, the ESS administrator and steering committee should periodically and systematically review the ESS with an eye toward improving it. Here's a list of possible revisions to consider:

► *Objectives.*

- [ ] Is the scope of the ESS still relevant?

- [ ] Should more ambitious objectives be pursued, perhaps by accelerating ESS processing of ideas?

- [ ] Should the type of ideas considered change, perhaps accepting ideas for new products and services?

► *Clarification.*

- [ ] Are there any rules or instructions that seem to cause misunderstandings?

- [ ] Can these be rewritten or otherwise clarified?

► *Eligibility.*

- [ ] Should more personnel be allowed to participate in the ESS?

- [ ] What about the extent to which supervisors and managers are allowed to submit ideas?

► *Effectiveness.*

- [ ] What are the common characteristics of ideas that *are* adopted?

- [ ] How can these characteristics be communicated throughout the organization to increase the percentage of submitted ideas that are ultimately adopted?

► *Efficiency.*

☐ Can the submission and evaluation process be streamlined?

☐ Is it possible for fewer people to be involved in the process?

☐ Can the forms and other paperwork be simplified?

☐ Is it time to computerize?

► *Awards.*

☐ Is the award structure still appropriate?

☐ Does it still provide sufficient motivation?

☐ Should additional awards be offered to supervisors, managers, evaluators and/or implementers?

IMPORTANT INFORMATION AHEAD

CONCLUDING TIPS AND OBSERVATIONS

To wrap up, here are a few concluding tips and observations to remember when building, implementing and running the ESS in your organization.

Teach Employees How to Be Creative

Many employees are naturally creative and will have no trouble submitting suggestions. But many employees must be taught how to be more creative. Use some of the idea-generation techniques described in Part III to grow their creativity.

Question Everything

Have employees get in the habit of constructively questioning everything they do. Many tasks are done simply because they have always been done, and done that way. Nobody has bothered to ask if they are still necessary. Everything should be questioned, and questioned often.

Realize That There Are Sacred Cows

In many organizations there are sacred cows that will not be subject to improvement by the suggestion program. This is, unfortunately, a fact of life. Being aware of this reality may save some frustration in the future.

Give Them Results

It is important to the long-term survival of the suggestion program that tangible results be produced quickly and continually thereafter. Everyone will be watching to see if the ESS delivers. An organized launch, executive management support, professional training and ongoing promotion are essential.

Remember the 80/20 Rule

The 80/20 rule applies to suggestion programs, too. You may find that 80% of the best suggestions come from 20% of the employee population. So make sure that repeat suggesters are treated well, but try also to expand your promotional efforts to involve the other 80%.

Let Them Down Easy

A 10–25% adoption rate is considered good for a suggestion program. Therefore, you will need to learn how to let people down easily when their suggestions aren't adopted. Explain it clearly, and leave them with a desire to submit more suggestions. It may help to let them know the adoption rate at your organization. This will demonstrate that they may have to submit several suggestions before one is adopted.

If You Don't Measure It, You Can't Control It

First, keep track of the number and types of improvement ideas submitted by employees. Otherwise, you will not be able to control them and reap the benefits. A formal suggestion program allows you to track and measure employee input. It also helps identify areas where employees have a low participation rate. Promotional efforts can be targeted at these low participation areas.

Second, teach employees to keep track of what they do. It is difficult to improve a process if it is not measured. For example, it is difficult to reduce the amount of time spent on a particular job if no one keeps track of the time currently spent.

CONCLUDING TIPS AND OBSERVATIONS (continued)

Be Prompt In Your Response

Quick response time is one of the most important elements of a successful suggestion program. Employees want to know what is happening with their suggestions throughout the evaluation process. Employees want an answer as soon as possible. Set a turnaround target for the ESS and give a final answer to suggesters within that time. A 30-day turnaround is a good goal for most ideas. If employees are informed, they won't lose interest in the program and stop submitting ideas.

It All Adds Up (Small Ideas Are Welcome)

Don't judge ideas too early or too quickly. What seems to be a small idea initially could turn out to be quite significant. Example: An idea estimated to save $1.00 a day, multiplied times 700 employees, times 260 working days a year, adds up to projected savings of $182,000! Give *all* ideas a chance to be evaluated and possibly implemented.

Give Managers a Piece of the Pie, Too

Managers are more likely to encourage and support their employees' suggestions if they know they will be rewarded for their employees' success. Try to incorporate rewards or recognition for managers based on the success of their staff.

Deal with the "That's Your Job" Personality

Some employees think that all ideas are part of every employee's job. That decision should be made by the employee's direct supervisor and the steering committee. This determination depends on how the organization handles the job-scope issue previously discussed.

Welcome Those Problem Spotters

There may be times when an employee has been able to spot a problem that needs to be solved, but does not have the solution. The program administrator should be available to help the employee create a solution to the problem. Encourage workers to let the program administrator know about problems, even if a solution has not yet been found.

Practice Makes Perfect

When conducting training sessions, have employees practice filling out an Employee Suggestion Form to get familiar with it.

Effectiveness Is Not Necessarily Uniqueness

Stress to employees that the ESS is asking for *effective* ideas, not necessarily *unique* ideas. Most changes have been thought of before, but nothing was done about it. This distinction is important, because employees or managers may say "I thought of that last year." Your response might be "Why didn't you do anything about it?" If workers' ideas lead to valuable changes, they should be rewarded whether the ideas were original or not. Of course, duplicate ideas do not fit under this category.

There's No Time Like the Present

While this book is still fresh on your mind, why not write up a tentative timetable for developing and implementing an ESS in your organization? Discuss the possibilities with your boss and then pick up the telephone. Arrange a meeting with management—if they're skeptical, go ahead and implement a Mini-ESS in your own office or department. You'll be glad you did.

Good luck!

PART

V

ESS
Forms

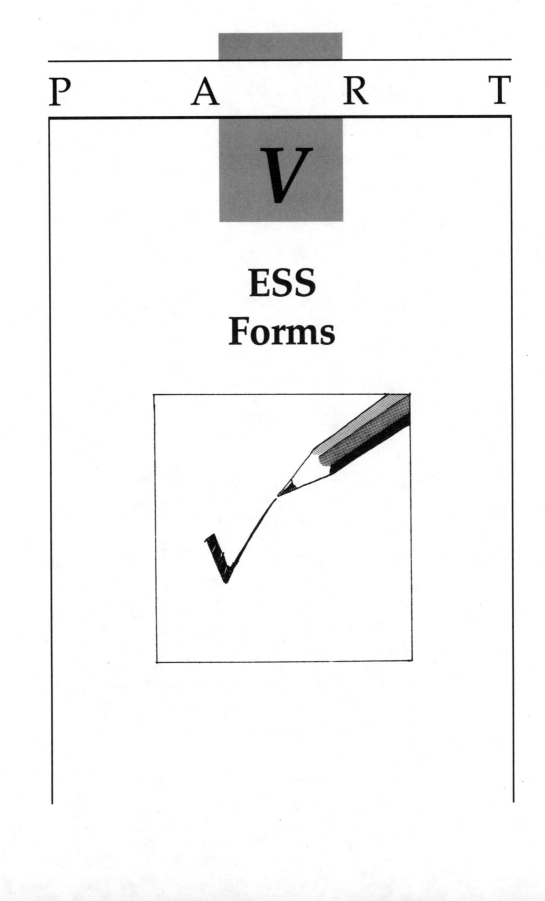

EMPLOYEE SUGGESTION FORM

(A COPY WILL BE RETURNED TO YOU AS AN ACKNOWLEDGMENT)

OFFICE USE ONLY	
Time/Date Received: _____	1. Type or print
	2. Attach additional pages if needed.
Suggestion Number: _____	3. Complete all sections, **SIGN** and **DATE** form. Suggestion will not be accepted if not signed by all suggesters.
Key Words: _____	4. **Send** the form and any attachments to the ESS office.
Evaluator: _____	5. A copy of this form with a suggestion number will be sent back to you as an acknowledgment.

Last Name (Print) First Initial	Position Title	Phone Number
Social Security Number Cost Center	Department	City

1. My Suggestion is. (State how and where it can be used, include drawings, sample forms.) _____

_____

_____

2. Describe Current Method, Procedure or Condition. (Be Specific) _____

_____

_____

3. Savings or Benefits. (Indicate how your suggestion will save money, time or other resources. What is your dollar estimate of savings for the first year or your suggestion?) _____

_____

_____

First year savings (Estimate) $ _____

I have read and agree to the rules printed on the backside of this form.

Signature(s) (All must sign/do not print)   S.S #   Date   Supervisor's Name

1. _____
2. _____
3. _____

(NOTE: This form may be copied without further permission from the publisher.)

IDEA EVALUATION FORM

Evaluation of Employee Suggestion, Adoption and Approval of Award

(Attach additional pages if needed)

EVALUATION OF IDEA		REFERENCE DATA
Name of Evaluator: _____	Dept. Name of Evaluator: _____	Suggestion No: _____
Evaluator Phone No: _____	Evaluator Location (City): _____	Date Received: _____
		Suggester Name: _____

SUMMARY OF EXPECTED BENEFITS

(Attach justification or explanation. For tangible benefits, attach detailed computations to justify summary figures. For intangible benefits, explain value and scope of application.)

TANGIBLE
(Estimated net benefits for first full year of operation after implementation)

COSTS	OLD METHOD	NEW METHOD	SAVINGS
Labor	$_____	$_____	$_____
Materials	$_____	$_____	$_____
TOTAL	$_____	$_____	$_____

INTANGIBLE

VALUE	SCOPE OF APPLICATION
☐ MODERATE	☐ LIMITED
☐ SUBSTANTIAL	☐ EXTENDED
☐ HIGH	☐ BROAD
☐ EXCEPTIONAL	☐ GENERAL

Is the idea within the suggester's normal job responsibilities, based on due consideration of his or her position description, assigned duties, position performance standards and the scope of application of the idea?

☐ YES   ☐ NO   Supervisor signature _____ Date _____

☐ Recommend adoption in whole (Date) _____

☐ Merits consideration by other offices (Specify)
Reason:

☐ Recommend adoption in part only (Specify)

☐ Recommend adoption for limited period (Begin ____ /End ____)

☐ Recommend Non-Adoption
Reason:

Signature of Evaluator: _____ Title of Evaluator: _____ Date: _____

AWARD RECOMMENDATION

FOR ESS OFFICE USE ONLY

Award Based on *Tangible* Benefits	Award Based on *Intangible* Benefits	Total Monetary Award:
$ _____	$ _____	$ _____

APPROVED BY: _____ DATE: _____

(NOTE: This form may be copied without further permission from the publisher.)

IDEA TRACKING LOG

R = Receipt Sent   E = Sent to Evaluator   A = Adopted   NA = Nonadopt

DATE	IDEA	R	E	A	NA	DATE CLOSED	NOTIFIED	SUGGESTER NAME & PHONE	EVALUATOR NAME & PHONE	TURN-AROUND # OF DAYS	AWARD AMOUNT

Assessment

EMPLOYEE SUGGESTION SYSTEMS

EMPLOYEE SUGGESTION SYSTEMS
BOOSTING PRODUCTIVITY AND PROFITS

A FIFTY-MINUTE™ BOOK

The objectives of this book are:

1. to point out benefits of an Employee Suggestion System.

2. to explain how to set up an Employee Suggestion System.

3. to discuss promotion ideas for an Employee Suggestion System.

4. to present ways to avoid problems with Employee Suggestion Systems.

Disclaimer:
These assessments were written to test the reader on the content of the book. They were not developed by a professional test writer. The publisher and author shall have neither liability nor responsibility to any person with respect to any loss or damage caused or alleged to be caused directly or indirectly by the assessment contained herein.

OBJECTIVE ASSESSMENT FOR EMPLOYEE SUGGESTION SYSTEMS

Select the best response.

1. Employees who are invested in their workplace
   A. enjoy work more.
   B. usually make meaningful contributions
   C. are likely to be committed to decisions they help shape.
   D. all of the above

2. Employee suggestion systems save U.S. businesses annually
   A. two million dollars
   B. ten million dollars.
   C. two billion dollars.
   D. ten billion dollars.

3. Without an ESS, useful suggestions may be
   A. blocked.
   B. neglected.
   C. discounted.
   D. all of the above

4. The more efficient use of equipment always
   A. encourages employee ideas.
   B. decreases overtime.
   C. saves power.
   D. decreases manual labor.

5. If employee suggestions are acted upon, employees will have
   A. improved morale.
   B. increased use of creativity.
   C. tangible and intangible rewards.
   D. all of the above

6. Employees can make the most practical suggestions about their work because they
   A. share ideas.
   B. enjoy volunteering ideas.
   C. are closest to it.
   D. understand management problems.

OBJECTIVE ASSESSMENT (continued)

7. If employees enjoy their jobs, a formal Employee Suggestion System (ESS) is unnecessary.
   A. True
   B. False

8. To be successful, an ESS
   A. should be created by employees.
   B. does not require written rules.
   C. must have the support of management.
   D. should be created by management.
   E. A and B

9. Steering committees of an ESS should
   A. represent the major functional areas of the organization.
   B. be balanced in other ways relevant to the organization.
   C. be selected from management.
   D. all of the above
   E. A and B

10. A wise strategic policy with a new ESS is to have
    A. ambitious objectives.
    B. modest objectives.

11. An ESS ensures that good ideas are
    A. funded.
    B. championed.
    C. not blocked by neglect or opponents.
    D. all of the above

12. All ideas should be eligible except those regarding
    A. other employees' compensation.
    B. reminders of policies not being followed.
    C. conditions of employment.
    D. all of the above
    E. A and C

13. A flat rather than a percentage award is recommended for
    A. nontraceable labor hours saved.
    B. team awards.
    C. intangible ideas.
    D. any of the above
    E. A and C

14. Team suggestions are best awarded by
    A. cash and merchandise points.
    B. travel and merchandise.

15. To encourage participation in the ESS,
    A. an appeals process should exist.
    B. all suggestions should receive some award.
    C. the ESS office should help fine-tune suggestions.
    D. all of the above
    E. A and C

16. Which ESS program name will be most likely to succeed?
    A. Employee-Generated Procedures
    B. Cost Containment System
    C. Quality Awards
    D. Bright Ideas

17. It is important for an organization to specify exactly how ESS ideas should be submitted and how they will be processed.
    A. True
    B. False

18. Managers are most likely to encourage ESS participation if they
    A. clearly understand the system.
    B. are provided with suggestion and evaluation forms.
    C. understand the rules and system flowchart.
    D. receive a percentage award for their employees' ideas.

19. To motivate participation in the ESS, management must
    A. provide rules and forms.
    B. promote it.
    C. train employees.
    D. believe in it.

20. It is very important that someone win a suggestion award
    A. every month.
    B. in every department.
    C. in the first few weeks.
    D. at even intervals.

OBJECTIVE ASSESSMENT (continued)

21. The ESS itself should
    A. not need to be improved.
    B. be reviewed regularly for possible improvement.

22. Trying to change some policies or procedures in some organizations may be impossible.
    A. True
    B. False

23. The usual percentage of ESS submitted ideas that cannot be adopted is
    A. 10–25%.
    B. 30–40%.
    C. 40–60%.
    D. 75–90%.

24. Response time to a suggestion should not be longer than about
    A. **one week.**
    B. one month.
    C. three months.
    D. six months.

25. If several people recognize an improvement need, the award should go to whomever
    A. recognizes the need.
    B. works out the solution.

Qualitative Objectives for *Employee Suggestion Systems*

To point out benefits of an Employee Suggestion System

Questions 1, 2, 3, 4, 5, 6, 7, 11

To explain how to set up an Employee Suggestion System

Questions 8, 9, 10, 12, 13, 14, 24

To discuss promotion ideas for an Employee Suggestion System

Questions 15, 16, 19, 20

To present ways to avoid problems with Employee Suggestion Systems

Questions 17, 18, 21, 22, 23, 25

ANSWER KEY

1. D	10. B	18. D
2. C	11. D	19. B
3. D	12. D	20. C
4. C	13. E	21. B
5. D	14. A	22. A
6. C	15. E	23. D
7. B	16. D	24. B
8. C	17. A	25. B
9. E		

Copyright © 1996, Crisp Publications, Inc.
1200 Hamilton Court
Menlo Park, California 94025

NOTES

NOTES

NOTES

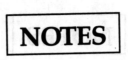

NOTES

NOTES

NOTES

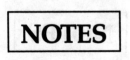

NOTES

NOW AVAILABLE FROM CRISP PUBLICATIONS

Books • Videos • CD Roms • Computer-Based Training Products

If you enjoyed this book, we have great news for you. There are over 200 books available in the *50-Minute*™ Series. To request a free full-line catalog, contact your local distributor or Crisp Publications, Inc., 1200 Hamilton Court, Menlo Park, CA 94025. Our toll-free number is 800-442-7477.

Subject Areas Include:

Management

Human Resources

Communication Skills

Personal Development

Marketing/Sales

Organizational Development

Customer Service/Quality

Computer Skills

Small Business and Entrepreneurship

Adult Literacy and Learning

Life Planning and Retirement

CRISP WORLDWIDE DISTRIBUTION

English language books are distributed worldwide. Major international distributors include:

ASIA/PACIFIC

Australia/New Zealand: In Learning, PO Box 1051 Springwood QLD, Brisbane, Australia 4127
Telephone: 7-3841-1061, Facsimile: 7-3841-1580   ATTN: Messrs. Gordon

Singapore: Graham Brash (Pvt) Ltd. 32, Gul Drive, Singapore 2262
Telphone: 65-861-1336, Facsimile: 65-861-4815   ATTN: Mr. Campbell

CANADA

Reid Publishing, Ltd., Box 69559-109 Thomas Street, Oakville, Ontario Canada L6J 7R4.
Telephone: (905) 842-4428, Facsimile: (905) 842-9327   ATTN: Mr. Reid

Trade Book Stores: Raincoast Books, 8680 Cambie Street, Vancouver, British Columbia, Canada V6P 6M9.
Telephone: (604) 323–7100, Facsimile: 604-323-2600   ATTN: Ms. Laidley

EUROPEAN UNION

England: Flex Training, Ltd. 9-15 Hitchin Street, Baldock, Hertfordshire, SG7 6A, England
Telephone: 1-462-896000, Facsimile: 1-462-892417   ATTN: Mr. Willetts

INDIA

Multi-Media HRD, Pvt., Ltd., National House, Tulloch Road, Appolo Bunder, Bombay, India 400-039
Telephone: 91-22-204-2281, Facsimile: 91-22-283-6478   ATTN: Messrs. Aggarwal

MIDDLE EAST

United Arab Emirates: Al-Mutanabbi Bookshop, PO Box 71946, Abu Dhabi
Telephone: 971-2-321-519, Facsimile: 971-2-317-706   ATTN: Mr. Salabbai

SOUTH AMERICA

Mexico: Grupo Editorial Iberoamerica, Serapio Rendon #125, Col. San Rafael, 06470 Mexico, D.F.
Telephone: 525-705-0585, Facsimile: 525-535-2009   ATTN: Señor Grepe

SOUTH AFRICA

Alternative Books, Unit A3 Sanlam Micro Industrial Park, Hammer Avenue STRYDOM Park, Randburg, 2194 South Africa
Telephone: 2711 792 7730, Facsimile: 2711 792 7787   ATTN: Mr. de Haas